Yo
H

2013

Aquarius

YOUR PERSONAL HOROSCOPE 2013

AQUARIUS

21st January–19th February

igloobooks.com

igloobooks
.com

This edition published by Igloo Books Ltd
Cottage Farm
Sywell
Northants
NN6 0BJ
www.igloobooks.com

Produced for Igloo Books by W. Foulsham & Co. Ltd, Capital Point, 33 Bath Road, Slough, Berkshire, SL1 3UF, England

VIV001 0712
2 4 6 8 10 9 7 5 3 1
ISBN: 978-0-85780-617-8

This is an abridged version of material originally published in Old Moore's Horoscope and Astral Diary.

Printed and manufactured in Malaysia

CONTENTS

INTRODUCTION

Your Personal Horoscopes have been specifically created to allow you to get the most from astrological patterns and the way they have a bearing on not only your zodiac sign, but nuances within it. Using the diary section of the book you can read about the influences and possibilities of each and every day of the year. It will be possible for you to see when you are likely to be cheerful and happy or those times when your nature is in retreat and you will be more circumspect. The diary will help to give you a feel for the specific 'cycles' of astrology and the way they can subtly change your day-to-day life. For example, when you see the sign ☿, this means that the planet Mercury is retrograde at that time. Retrograde means it appears to be running backwards through the zodiac. Such a happening has a significant effect on communication skills, but this is only one small aspect of how the Personal Horoscope can help you.

With Your Personal Horoscope the story doesn't end with the diary pages. It includes simple ways for you to work out the zodiac sign the Moon occupied at the time of your birth, and what this means for your personality. In addition, if you know the time of day you were born, it is possible to discover your Ascendant, yet another important guide to your personal make-up and potential.

Many readers are interested in relationships and in knowing how well they get on with people of other astrological signs. You might also be interested in the way you appear to very different sorts of individuals. If you are such a person, the section on Venus will be of particular interest. Despite the rapidly changing position of this planet, you can work out your Venus sign, and learn what bearing it will have on your life.

Using Your Personal Horoscope you can travel on one of the most fascinating and rewarding journeys that anyone can take – the journey to a better realisation of self.

THE ESSENCE OF AQUARIUS

Exploring the Personality of Aquarius the Water Carrier

(21ST JANUARY – 19TH FEBRUARY)

What's in a sign?

Oh, what a wonderful person you can be! Despite a number of contradictions and one of the most complicated natures to be found anywhere in the zodiac, you certainly know how to make friends and influence people. Your ruling planet is Uranus, one of the more recently discovered members of the solar system's family. It rules modern communications, such as radio and television, and also has a response to the recent discoveries of science. It is within the world of 'the modern' that you reside and you have little or no difficulty keeping up with the ever-increasing pace of life.

People naturally like you and it's not surprising. You are open, liberal, and rarely judgmental, and you are often surrounded by deeply original and even eccentric types. Life to you is a storybook full of fascinating tales. Aquarians amass information 'on the hoof' and very little passes you by. Understanding what makes others tick is meat and drink to you and proves to be a source of endless joy. Unlike the other Air signs of Gemini and Libra, you are able to spend long hours on your own if necessary and always keep your mind active.

Aquarians have great creative potential; they are refined, often extremely well educated and they remain totally classless. This makes it easy for you to get on with just about any sort of person and also explains your general success in the material world. You are fascinating, original, thought-provoking and even quite deep on occasions. Matters that take months for others to synthesise, you can absorb in minutes. It is clear to everyone that you are one of life's natural leaders, but when you head any organisation you do so by co-operation and example because you are not in the least authoritarian.

In love you can be ardent and sincere – for a while at least. You need to be loved and it's true that deeply personal relationships can be a problem to you if they are not supplying what is most important to you. Few people know the real you, because your nature exists on so many different levels. For this reason alone you defy analysis and tend to remain outside the scope of orthodoxy. And because people can't weigh you up adequately, you appear to be more fascinating than ever.

Aquarius resources

Your chief resource has to be originality. Like a precious Fabergé Egg you are a single creation, unique and quite unlike anything else to be found anywhere in the world. Of course, used wrongly, this can make you seem odd or even downright peculiar. But Aquarians usually have a knack for creating the best possible impression. The chances are that you dress in your own way and speak the words that occur to you, and that you have a side to your nature that shuns convention. Despite this you know how to adapt when necessary. As a result your dinner parties would sport guests of a wide variety of types and stations. All of these people think they know the 'real you' and remain committed to helping you as much as they can.

The natural adaptability that goes along with being an Aquarian makes it possible for you to turn your hand to many different projects. And because you are from an Air sign, you can undertake a variety of tasks at the same time. This makes for a busy life, but being on the go is vital for you and you only tire when you are forced into jobs that you find demeaning, pointless or downright dull.

All of the above combines to make a nature that has 'resourcefulness' as its middle name. Arriving at a given set of circumstances – say a specific task that has to be undertaken – you first analyse what is required. Having done so you get cracking and invariably manage to impress all manner of people with your dexterity, attention to detail and downright intelligence. You can turn work into a social event, or derive financial gain from your social life. Activity is the keyword and you don't really differentiate between the various components of life as many people would.

Success depends on a number of different factors. You need to be doing things you enjoy as much you can and you simply cannot be held back or bound to follow rules that appear to make no sense to you. You respond well to kindness, and generally receive it because you are so considerate yourself. But perhaps your greatest skill of all is your ability to make a silk purse out of a sow's ear. You are never stuck for an idea and rarely let financial restrictions get in your way.

Beneath the surface

'What you see is what you get' could never really be considered a sensible or accurate statement when applied to the sign of Aquarius. It's difficult enough for you to know the way your complicated mind works, and almost impossible for others to sort out the tangle of possibilities. Your mind can be as untidy as a tatty workbox on occasions and yet at other times you can see through situations with a clarity that would dazzle almost any observer. It really depends on a whole host of circumstances, some of which are inevitably beyond your own control. You are at your best when you are allowed to take charge from the very start of any project, because then your originality of thought comes into play. Your sort of logic is unique to you, so don't expect anyone else to go down the same mental routes that you find easy to follow.

Aquarians are naturally kind and don't tend to discriminate. This is not a considered matter, it's simply the way you are. As a result it is very hard for you to understand prejudice, or individuals who show any form of intolerance. The fairness that you exemplify isn't something that you have to work at – it comes as naturally to you as breathing does.

You can be very peculiar and even a little cranky on occasions. These aspects of your nature are unlikely to have any bearing on your overall popularity, but they do betray a rather unusual mindset that isn't like that of any other zodiac sign. When you feel stressed you tend to withdraw into yourself, which is not really good for you. A much better strategy would be to verbalise what you are thinking, even though this is not always particularly easy to do.

There are many people in the world who think they know you well, but each and every one of them knows only one Aquarian. There are always more, each a unique individual and probably as much of a mystery to you as they would be to all your relatives and friends, that is if any of them suspected just how deep and mysterious you can be. Despite these facts, your mind is clear and concise, enabling you to get to the truth of any given situation almost immediately. You should never doubt your intuitive foresight and, in the main, must always back your hunches. It is rare indeed for you to be totally wrong about the outcome of any potential situation and your genuine originality of thought is the greatest gift providence has bestowed on you.

Making the best of yourself

Interacting with the world is most important to you. Although you can sometimes be a good deal quieter than the other Air signs of Gemini and Libra, you are still a born communicator, with a great need to live your life to the full. If you feel hemmed in or constrained by circumstances, you are not going to show your best face to family, friends or colleagues. That's why you must move heaven and earth to make certain that you are not tied down in any way. Maintaining a sense of freedom is really just a mental state to Aquarius but it is absolutely vital to your well-being.

As far as work is concerned you need to be doing something that allows you the room you need to move. Any occupation that means thinking on your feet would probably suit you fine. All the same you feel more comfortable in administrative surroundings, rather than getting your hands dirty. Any profession that brings change and variety on a daily basis would be best. You are a good team operator, and yet can easily lead from the front. Don't be frightened to show colleagues that you have an original way of looking at life and that you are an inveterate problem solver.

In terms of friendship you tend to be quite catholic in your choice of pals. Making the best of yourself means keeping things that way. You are not naturally jealous yourself but you do tend to attract friends who are. Make it plain that you can't tie yourself down to any one association, no matter how old or close it may be. At least if you do this nobody can suggest that they weren't warned when you wander off to talk to someone else. Personal relationships are a different matter, though it's hardly likely that you would live in the pocket of your partner. In any situation you need space to breathe, and this includes romantic attachments. People who know you well will not try to hem you in.

Don't be frightened to show your unconventional, even wild side to the world at large. You are a bold character, with a great deal to say and a natural warmth that could melt an iceberg. This is the way providence made you and it is only right to use your gifts to the full.

The impressions you give

You are not a naturally secretive person and don't hold back very much when it comes to speaking your mind. It might be suggested therefore that the external and internal Aquarian is more or less the same person. Although generally true, it has to be remembered that you have a multi-faceted nature and one that adapts quickly to changing circumstances. It is this very adaptability that sets you apart in the eyes of the world.

You often make decisions based on intuitive foresight and although many Aquarians are of above average intelligence, you won't always make use of a deep knowledge of any given situation. In essence you often do what seems right, though you tend to act whilst others are still standing around and thinking. This makes you good to have around in a crisis and convinces many of those looking on that you are incredibly capable, relaxed and confident. Of course this isn't always the case, but even a nervous interior tends to breed outward action in the case of your zodiac sign, so the world can be forgiven for jumping to the wrong conclusion.

People like you – there's no doubt about that. However, you must realise that you have a very upfront attitude, which on occasions is going to get you into trouble. Your occasional weirdness, rather than being a turn-off, is likely to stimulate the interest that the world has in you. Those with whom you come into contract invariably find your personality to be attractive, generous, high-spirited and refreshing. For all these reasons it is very unlikely that you would actually make many enemies, even if some folk are clearly jealous of the easy way you have with the world.

One of the great things about Aquarians is that they love to join in. As a result you may find yourself doing all sorts of things that others would find either difficult or frightening. You can be zany, wild and even mad on occasions, but these tendencies will only get you liked all the more. The world will only tire of you if you allow yourself to get down in the dumps or grumpy – a very rare state for Aquarius.

The way forward

In terms of living your life to the full it is probable that you don't need any real advice from an astrologer. Your confidence allows you to go places that would make some people shiver, whilst your intuitive foresight gives you the armoury you need to deal with a world that can sometimes seem threatening. Yet for all this you are not immune to mental turmoil on occasions, and probably spend rather too much time in the fast lane. It's good to rest, a fact that you need to remember the next time you find yourself surrounded by twenty-seven jobs, all of which you are trying to undertake at the same time.

The more the world turns in the direction of information technology, the happier you are likely to become. If others have difficulty in this age of computers, it's likely that you relish the challenges and the opportunities that these artificial intelligences offer. You are happy with New Age concepts and tend to look at the world with compassion and understanding. Despite the fact that you are always on the go, it's rare for you to be moving forward so fast that you forget either the planet that brought you to birth, or the many underprivileged people who inhabit parts of it. You have a highly developed conscience and tend to work for the good of humanity whenever you can.

You might not be constructed of the highest moral fibre known to humanity, a fact that sometimes shows when it comes to romantic attachments. Many Aquarians play the field at some time in their lives and it's certain that you need a personal relationship that keeps you mentally stimulated. Although your exterior can sometimes seem superficial, you have a deep and sensitive soul – so perhaps you should marry a poet, or at least someone who can cope with the twists and turns of the Aquarian mind. Aquarians who tie themselves down too early, or to the wrong sort of individual, invariable end up regretting the fact.

You can be deeply creative and need to live in clean and cheerful surroundings. Though not exactly a minimalist you don't like clutter and constantly need to spring-clean your home – and your mind. Living with others isn't difficult for you, in fact it's essential. Since you are so adaptable you fit in easily to almost any environment, though you will always ultimately stamp your own character onto it. You love to be loved and offer a great deal in return, even if you are occasionally absent when people need you the most. In essence you are in love with life and so perhaps you should not be too surprised to discover that it is very fond of you too.

AQUARIUS ON THE CUSP

Astrological profiles are altered for those people born at either the beginning or the end of a zodiac sign, or, more properly, on the cusps of a sign. In the case of Aquarius this would be on the 21st of January and for two or three days after, and similarly at the end of the sign, probably from the 17th to the 19th of February.

The Capricorn Cusp – January 21st to 23rd

What really sets you apart is a genuinely practical streak that isn't always present in the sign of Aquarius when taken alone. You are likely to have all the joy of life and much of the devil-may-care attitude of your Sun sign, but at the same time you are capable of getting things done in a very positive way. This makes you likely to achieve a higher degree of material success and means that you ally managerial skills with the potential for rolling up your sleeves and taking part in the 'real work' yourself. Alongside this you are able to harness the naturally intuitive qualities of Aquarius in a very matter-of-fact way. Few people would have the ability to pull the wool over your eyes and you are rarely stuck for a solution, even to apparently difficult problems.

You express yourself less well than Aquarius taken alone, and you may have a sort of reserve that leads others to believe that your mind is full of still waters which run very deep. The air of mystery can actually be quite useful, because it masks an ability to react and move quickly when necessary, which is a great surprise to the people around you. However, there are two sides to every coin and if there is a slightly negative quality to this cuspid position it might lie in the fact that you are not quite the communicator that tends to be the case with Aquarius, and you could go through some fairly quiet and introspective phases that those around you would find somewhat difficult to understand. In a positive sense this offers a fairly wistful aspect to your nature that may, in romantic applications, appear very attractive. There is something deeply magnetic about your nature and it isn't quite possible for everyone to understand what makes you tick. Actually this is part of your appeal because there is nothing like curiosity on the part of others to enhance your profile.

Getting things done is what matters the most to you, harnessed to the ability to see the wider picture in life. It's true that not everyone understands your complex nature, but in friendship you are scarcely short of supportive types. Family members can be especially important to you and personal attachments are invariably made for life.

The Pisces Cusp – February 17th to 19th

It appears that you are more of a thinker than most and achieve depths of contemplation that would be totally alien to some signs of the zodiac. Much of your life is given over to the service you show for humanity as a whole but you don't sink into the depths of despair in the way that some Piscean individuals are inclined to do. You are immensely likeable and rarely stuck for a good idea. You know how to enjoy yourself, even if this quality is usually tied to the support and assistance that you constantly give to those around you.

Many of you will already have chosen a profession that somehow fulfils your need to be of service, and it isn't unusual for Pisces-cusp Aquarians to alter their path in life totally if it isn't fulfilling this most basic requirement. When necessary, you can turn your hand to almost anything, generally giving yourself totally to the task in hand, sometimes to the exclusion of everything else. People with this combination often have two very different sorts of career, sometimes managing to do both at the same time. Confidence in practical matters isn't usually lacking, even if you sometimes think that your thought processes are a little bit muddled.

In love you are ardent and more sincere than Aquarius sometimes seems to be. There can be a tinge of jealousy at work now and again in deep relationships, but you are less likely than Pisces to let this show. You tend to be very protective of the people who are most important in your life and these are probably fewer in number than often seems to be the case for Aquarius. Your love of humanity and the needs it has of you are of supreme importance and you barely let a day pass without offering some sort of assistance. For this reason, and many others, you are a much loved individual and show your most caring face to the world for the majority of your life. Material success can be hard to come by at first, but it isn't really an aspect of life that worries you too much in any case. It is far more important for you to be content with your lot and, if you are happy, it seems that more or less everything else tends to follow.

AQUARIUS AND ITS ASCENDANTS

The nature of every individual on the planet is composed of the rich variety of zodiac signs and planetary positions that were present at the time of their birth. Your Sun sign, which in your case is Aquarius, is one of the many factors when it comes to assessing the unique person you are. Probably the most important consideration, other than your Sun sign, is to establish the zodiac sign that was rising over the eastern horizon at the time that you were born. This is your Ascending or Rising sign. Most popular astrology fails to take account of the Ascendant, and yet its importance remains with you from the very moment of your birth, through every day of your life. The Ascendant is evident in the way you approach the world, and so, when meeting a person for the first time, it is this astrological influence that you are most likely to notice first. Our Ascending sign essentially represents what we appear to be, while the Sun sign is what we feel inside ourselves.

The Ascendant also has the potential for modifying our overall nature. For example, if you were born at a time of day when Aquarius was passing over the eastern horizon (this would be around the time of dawn) then you would be classed as a double Aquarian. As such, you would typify this zodiac sign, both internally and in your dealings with others. However, if your Ascendant sign turned out to be a Fire sign, such as Aries, there would be a profound alteration of nature, away from the expected qualities of Aquarius.

One of the reasons why popular astrology often ignores the Ascendant is that it has always been rather difficult to establish. We have found a way to make this possible by devising an easy-to-use table, which you will find on page 157 of this book. Using this, you can establish your Ascendant sign at a glance. You will need to know your rough time of birth, then it is simply a case of following the instructions.

For those readers who have no idea of their time of birth it might be worth allowing a good friend, or perhaps your partner, to read through the section that follows this introduction. Someone who deals with you on a regular basis may easily discover your Ascending sign, even though you could have some difficulty establishing it for yourself. A good understanding of this component of your nature is essential if you want to be aware of that 'other person' who is responsible for the way you make contact with the world at large. Your Sun sign, Ascendant sign, and the other pointers in this book will, together, allow you a far better understanding of what makes you tick as an individual. Peeling back the different layers of your astrological make-up can be an enlightening experience, and the Ascendant may represent one of the most important layers of all.

Aquarius with Aquarius Ascendant

You are totally unique and quite original, so much so that very few people could claim to understand what makes you tick. Routines get on your nerves and you need to be out there doing something most of the time. Getting where you want to go in life isn't too difficult, except that when you arrive, your destination might not look half so interesting as it did before. You are well liked and should have many friends. This is not to say that your pals have much in common with each other, because you choose from a wide cross-section of people. Although folks see you as being very reasonable in the main, you are capable of being quite cranky on occasions. Your intuition is extremely strong and is far less likely to let you down than would be the case with some individuals.

Travel is very important to you and you will probably live for some time in a different part of your own country, or even in another part of the world. At work you are more than capable, but do need something to do that you find personally stimulating, because you are not very good at constant routine. You can be relied upon to use your originality and find solutions that are instinctive and brilliant. Most people are very fond of you.

Aquarius with Pisces Ascendant

Here we find the originality of Aquarius balanced by the very sensitive qualities of Pisces, and it makes for a very interesting combination. When it comes to understanding other people you are second to none, but it's certain that you are more instinctive than either Pisces or Aquarius when taken alone. You are better at routines than Aquarius, but also relish a challenge more than the typical Piscean would. Active and enterprising, you tend to know what you want from life, but consideration of others, and the world at large, will always be part of the scenario. People with this combination often work on behalf of humanity and are to be found in social work, the medical profession and religious institutions. As far as beliefs are concerned you don't conform to established patterns, and yet may get closer to the truth of the Creator than many deep theological thinkers have ever been able to do. Acting on impulse as much as you do means that not everyone understands the way your mind works, but your popularity will invariably see you through.

Passionate and deeply sensitive, you are able to negotiate the twists and turns of a romantic life that is hardly likely to be run-of-the-mill. In the end, however, you should be able to discover a very deep personal and spiritual happiness.

Aquarius with Aries Ascendant

If ever anyone could be accused of setting off immediately, but slowly, it has to be you. These are very contradictory signs and the differences will express themselves in a variety of ways. One thing is certain, you have tremendous tenacity and will see a job through patiently from beginning to end, without tiring on the way and ensuring that every detail is taken care of properly. This combination often brings good health and a great capacity for continuity, particularly in terms of the length of life. You are certainly not as argumentative as the typical Aries, but you do know how to get your own way, which is just as well because you are usually thinking on behalf of everyone else and not just on your own account.

At home you can relax, which is a blessing for Aries, though in fact you seldom choose to do so because you always have some project or other on the go. You probably enjoy knocking down and rebuilding walls, though this is a practical tendency and not responsive to relationships, in which you are ardent and sincere. Impetuosity is as close to your heart as is the case for any type of subject, though you certainly have the ability to appear patient and steady. But it's just a front, isn't it?

Aquarius with Taurus Ascendant

There is nothing that you fail to think about deeply and with great intensity. You are wise, honest and very scientific in your approach to life. Routines are necessary in life but you have most of them sorted out well in advance and so always have time to look at the next interesting fact. If you don't spend all your time watching documentaries on the television set, you make a good friend and love to socialise. Most of the great discoveries of the world were probably made by people with this sort of astrological combination, though your nature is rather 'odd' on occasions and so can be rather difficult for others to understand.

You may be most surprised when others tell you that you are eccentric, but you don't really mind too much because for half of the time you are not inhabiting the same world as the rest of us. Because you can be delightfully dotty you are probably much loved and cherished by your friends, of which there are likely to be many. Family members probably adore you too, and you can be guaranteed to entertain anyone with whom you come into contact. The only fly in the ointment is that you sometimes lose track of reality, whatever that might be, and fly high in your own atmosphere of rarefied possibilities.

Aquarius with Gemini Ascendant

If you were around in the 1960s there is every chance that you were the first to go around with flowers in your hair. You are unconventional, original, quirky and entertaining. Few people would fail to notice your presence and you take life as it comes, even though on most occasions you are firmly in the driving seat. It all probability you care very much about the planet on which you live and the people with whom you share it. Not everyone understands you, but that does not really matter, for you have more than enough communication skills to put your message across intact. You should avoid wearing yourself out by worrying about things that you cannot control, and you definitely gain from taking time out to meditate. However, whether or not you allow yourself that luxury remains to be seen.

If you are not the most communicative form of Gemini subject then you must come a close second. Despite this fact much of what you have to say makes real sense and you revel in the company of interesting, intelligent and stimulating people, whose opinions on a host of matters will add to your own considerations. You are a true original in every sense of the word and the mere fact of your presence in the world is bound to add to the enjoyment of life experienced by the many people with whom you make contact.

Aquarius with Cancer Ascendant

The truly original spark, for which the sign of Aquarius is famed, can only enhance the caring qualities of Cancer, and is also inclined to bring the Crab out of its shell to a much greater extent than would be the case with certain other zodiac combinations. Aquarius is a party animal and never arrives without something interesting to say, which is doubly the case when the reservoir of emotion and consideration that is Cancer is feeding the tap. Your nature can be rather confusing for even you to deal with, but you are inspirational, bright, charming and definitely fun to be around.

The Cancer element in your nature means that you care about your home and the people to whom you are related. You are also a good and loyal friend, who would keep attachments for much longer than could be expected for Aquarius alone. You love to travel and can be expected to make many journeys to far-off places during your life. Some attention will have to be paid to your health, because you are capable of burning up masses of nervous energy, often without getting the periods of rest and contemplation that are essential to the deeper qualities of the sign of Cancer. Nevertheless you have determination, resilience and a refreshing attitude that lifts the spirits of the people in your vicinity.

Aquarius with Leo Ascendant

All associations with Aquarius bring originality, and you are no exception. You aspire to do your best most of the time but manage to achieve your objectives in an infinitely amusing and entertaining way. Not that you set out to do so, because if you are an actor on the stage of life, it seems as though you are a natural one. There is nothing remotely pretentious about your breezy personality or your ability to occupy the centre of any stage. This analogy is quite appropriate because you probably like the theatre. Being in any situation when reality is suspended for a while suits you down to the ground, and in any case you may regularly ask yourself if you even recognise what reality is. Always asking questions, both of yourself and the world at large, you soldier on relentlessly, though not to the exclusion of having a good time on the way.

Keeping to tried and tested paths is not your way. You are a natural trailblazer who is full of good ideas and who has the energy to put them into practice. You care deeply for the people who play an important part in your life but are wise enough to allow them the space they need to develop their own personalities along the way. Most people like you, many love you, and one or two think that you really are the best thing since sliced bread.

Aquarius with Virgo Ascendant

How could anyone make the convention unconventional? Well, if anyone can manage, you can. There are great contradictions here, because on the one hand you always want to do the expected thing, but the Aquarian quality within your nature loves to surprise everyone on the way. If you don't always know what you are thinking or doing, it's a pretty safe bet that others won't either, so it's important on occasions really to stop and think. However this is not a pressing concern, because you tend to live a fairly happy life and muddle through no matter what. Other people tend to take to you well and it is likely that you will have many friends. You tend to be bright and cheerful and can approach even difficult tasks with the certainty that you have the skills necessary to see them through to their conclusion. Give and take are important factors in the life of any individual and particularly so in your case. Because you can stretch yourself in order to understand what makes other people think and act in the way that they do, you have the reputation of being a good friend and a reliable colleague.

In love you can be somewhat more fickle than the typical Virgoan, and yet you are always interesting to live with. Where you are, things happen, and you mix a sparkling wit with deep insights.

Aquarius with Libra Ascendant

Stand by for a truly interesting and very inspiring combination here, but one that is sometimes rather difficult to fathom, even for the sort of people who believe themselves to be very perceptive. The reason for this could be that any situation has to be essentially fixed and constant in order to get a handle on it, and this is certainly not the case for the Aquarian–Libran type. The fact is that both these signs are Air signs, and to a certain extent as unpredictable as the wind itself.

To most people you seem to be original, frank, free and very outspoken. Not everything you do makes sense to others and if you were alive during the hippy era, it is likely that you went around with flowers in your hair, for you are a free-thinking idealist at heart. With age you mature somewhat, but never too much, because you will always see the strange, the comical and the original in life. This is what keeps you young and is one of the factors that makes you so very attractive to members of the opposite sex. Many people will want to 'adopt' you and you are at your very best when in company. Much of your effort is expounded on others and yet, unless you discipline yourself a good deal, personal relationships of the romantic sort can bring certain difficulties. Careful planning is necessary.

Aquarius with Scorpio Ascendant

Here we have a combination that shows much promise and a flexibility that allows many changes in direction, allied to a power to succeed, sometimes very much against all the odds. Aquarius lightens the load of the Scorpio mind, turning the depths into potential, and intuitive foresight into a means for getting on in life. There are depths here, because even airy Aquarius isn't so easy to understand, and it is therefore a fact that some people with this combination will always be something of a mystery. However, even this fact can be turned to your advantage because it means that people will always be looking at you. Confidence is so often the key to success in life and the Scorpio–Aquarius mix offers this, or at least appears to do so. Even when this is not entirely the case, the fact that everyone around you believes it to be true is often enough.

You are usually good to know, and show a keen intellect and a deep intelligence, aided by a fascination for life that knows no bounds. When at your best you are giving, understanding, balanced and active. On those occasions when things are not going well for you, beware of a stubborn streak and the need to be sensational. Keep it light and happy and you won't go far wrong. Most of you are very, very much loved.

Aquarius with Sagittarius Ascendant

There is an original streak to your nature which is very attractive to the people with whom you share your life. Always different, ever on the go and anxious to try out the next experiment in life, you are interested in almost everything, and yet deeply attached to almost nothing. Everyone you know thinks that you are a little 'odd', but you probably don't mind them believing this because you know it to be true. In fact it is possible that you positively relish your eccentricity, which sets you apart from the common herd and means that you are always going to be noticed.

Although it may seem strange with this combination of Air and Fire, you can be distinctly cool on occasions, have a deep and abiding love of your own company now and again and won't be easily understood. Love comes fairly easily to you but there are times when you are accused of being self-possessed, self-indulgent and not willing enough to fall in line with the wishes of those around you. Despite this you walk on and on down your own path. At heart you are an extrovert and you love to party, often late into the night. Luxury appeals to you, though it tends to be of the transient sort. Travel could easily play a major and a very important part in your life.

Aquarius with Capricorn Ascendant

Here the determination of Capricorn is assisted by a slightly more adaptable quality and an off-beat personality that tends to keep everyone else guessing. You don't care to be quite so predictable as the archetypal Capricorn would be, and there is a more idealistic quality here, or at least one that shows more. A greater number of friends than Capricorn usually keeps is likely, though less than the true Aquarian would gather. Few people doubt your sincerity, though by no means all of them understand what makes you tick. Unfortunately you are not in a position to help them out, because you are not too sure yourself. All the same, you muddle through and can be very capable when the mood takes you.

Being a natural traveller, you love to see new places and would be quite fascinated by cultures that are very different to your own. People with this combination are inclined to spend some time living abroad and may even settle there. You look out for the underdog and will always have time for a good cause, no matter what it takes to help. In romantic terms you are a reliable partner, though with a slightly wayward edge which, if anything, tends to make you even more attractive. Listen to your intuition, which is well honed and rarely lets you down. Generally speaking you are very popular.

THE MOON AND THE PART IT PLAYS IN YOUR LIFE

In astrology the Moon is probably the single most important heavenly body after the Sun. Its unique position, as partner to the Earth on its journey around the solar system, means that the Moon appears to pass through the signs of the zodiac extremely quickly. The zodiac position of the Moon at the time of your birth plays a great part in personal character and is especially significant in the build-up of your emotional nature.

Your Own Moon Sign

Discovering the position of the Moon at the time of your birth has always been notoriously difficult because tracking the complex zodiac positions of the Moon is not easy. This process has been reduced to three simple stages with our Lunar Tables. A breakdown of the Moon's zodiac positions can be found from page 35 onwards, so that once you know what your Moon Sign is, you can see what part this plays in the overall build-up of your personal character.

If you follow the instructions on the next page you will soon be able to work out exactly what zodiac sign the Moon occupied on the day that you were born and you can then go on to compare the reading for this position with those of your Sun sign and your Ascendant. It is partly the comparison between these three important positions that goes towards making you the unique individual you are.

HOW TO DISCOVER YOUR MOON SIGN

This is a three-stage process. You may need a pen and a piece of paper but if you follow the instructions below the process should only take a minute or so.

STAGE 1 First of all you need to know the Moon Age at the time of your birth. If you look at Moon Table 1, on page 33, you will find all the years between 1915 and 2013 down the left side. Find the year of your birth and then trace across to the right to the month of your birth. Where the two intersect you will find a number. This is the date of the New Moon in the month that you were born. You now need to count forward the number of days between the New Moon and your own birthday. For example, if the New Moon in the month of your birth was shown as being the 6th and you were born on the 20th, your Moon Age Day would be 14. If the New Moon in the month of your birth came after your birthday, you need to count forward from the New Moon in the previous month, which, if you were born in January, means you must look at December in the previous year. You cannot count from December in the year of your birth, as that month is *after* your birth. Whatever the result, jot this number down so that you do not forget it.

STAGE 2 Take a look at Moon Table 2 on page 34. Down the left hand column look for the date of your birth. Now trace across to the month of your birth. Where the two meet you will find a letter. Copy this letter down alongside your Moon Age Day.

STAGE 3 Moon Table 3 on page 34 will supply you with the zodiac sign the Moon occupied on the day of your birth. Look for your Moon Age Day down the left hand column and then for the letter you found in Stage 2. Where the two converge you will find a zodiac sign and this is the sign occupied by the Moon on the day that you were born.

Your Zodiac Moon Sign Explained

You will find a profile of all zodiac Moon Signs on pages 35 to 38, showing in yet another way how astrology helps to make you into the individual that you are. In each daily entry of the Astral Diary you can find the zodiac position of the Moon for every day of the year. This also allows you to discover your lunar birthdays. Since the Moon passes through all the signs of the zodiac in about a month, you can expect something like twelve lunar birthdays each year. At these times you are likely to be emotionally steady and able to make the sort of decisions that have real, lasting value.

MOON TABLE 1

YEAR	DEC	JAN	FEB	YEAR	DEC	JAN	FEB	YEAR	DEC	JAN	FEB
1915	6	15	14	1948	1/30	11	9	1981	26	6	4
1916	25	5	3	1949	19	29	27	1982	15	25	23
1917	13	24	22	1950	9	18	16	1983	4	14	13
1918	2	12	11	1951	28	7	6	1984	22	3	1
1919	21	1/31	–	1952	17	26	25	1985	12	21	19
1920	10	20	19	1953	6	15	14	1986	1/30	10	9
1921	29	9	8	1954	25	5	3	1987	20	29	28
1922	18	27	26	1955	14	24	22	1988	9	19	17
1923	8	17	15	1956	2	13	11	1989	28	7	6
1924	26	6	5	1957	21	1/30	–	1990	17	26	25
1925	15	24	23	1958	10	19	18	1991	6	15	14
1926	5	14	12	1959	29	9	7	1992	24	4	3
1927	24	3	2	1960	18	27	26	1993	14	23	22
1928	12	21	19	1961	7	16	15	1994	2	11	10
1929	1/30	11	9	1962	26	6	5	1995	22	1/30	–
1930	19	29	28	1963	15	25	23	1996	10	20	18
1931	9	18	17	1964	4	14	13	1997	28	9	7
1932	27	7	6	1965	22	3	1	1998	18	27	26
1933	17	25	24	1966	12	21	19	1999	7	17	16
1934	6	15	14	1967	1/30	10	9	2000	26	6	4
1935	25	5	3	1968	20	29	28	2001	15	25	23
1936	13	24	22	1969	9	19	17	2002	4	13	12
1937	2	12	11	1970	28	7	6	2003	23	3	1
1938	21	1/31	–	1971	17	26	25	2004	11	21	20
1939	10	20	19	1972	6	15	14	2005	30	10	9
1940	28	9	8	1973	25	5	4	2006	20	29	28
1941	18	27	26	1974	14	24	22	2007	9	18	16
1942	8	16	15	1975	3	12	11	2008	27	8	6
1943	27	6	4	1976	21	1/31	29	2009	16	26	25
1944	15	25	24	1977	10	19	18	2010	6	15	14
1945	4	14	12	1978	29	9	7	2011	25	4	3
1946	23	3	2	1979	18	27	26	2012	12	23	22
1947	12	21	19	1980	7	16	15	2013	2	12	10

TABLE 2

DAY	JAN	FEB
1	A	D
2	A	D
3	A	D
4	A	D
5	A	D
6	A	D
7	A	D
8	A	D
9	A	D
10	A	E
11	B	E
12	B	E
13	B	E
14	B	E
15	B	E
16	B	E
17	B	E
18	B	E
19	B	E
20	B	F
21	C	F
22	C	F
23	C	F
24	C	F
25	C	F
26	C	F
27	C	F
28	C	F
29	C	F
30	C	–
31	D	–

MOON TABLE 3

M/D	A	B	C	D	E	F	G
0	CP	AQ	AQ	AQ	PI	PI	PI
1	AQ	AQ	AQ	PI	PI	PI	AR
2	AQ	AQ	PI	PI	PI	AR	AR
3	AQ	PI	PI	PI	AR	AR	AR
4	PI	PI	AR	AR	AR	AR	TA
5	PI	AR	AR	AR	TA	TA	TA
6	AR	AR	AR	TA	TA	TA	GE
7	AR	AR	TA	TA	TA	GE	GE
8	AR	TA	TA	TA	GE	GE	GE
9	TA	TA	GE	GE	GE	CA	CA
10	TA	GE	GE	GE	CA	CA	CA
11	GE	GE	GE	CA	CA	CA	LE
12	GE	GE	CA	CA	CA	LE	LE
13	GE	CA	CA	LE	LE	LE	LE
14	CA	CA	LE	LE	LE	VI	VI
15	CA	LE	LE	LE	VI	VI	VI
16	LE	LE	LE	VI	VI	VI	LI
17	LE	LE	VI	VI	VI	LI	LI
18	LE	VI	VI	VI	LI	LI	LI
19	VI	VI	VI	LI	LI	LI	SC
20	VI	LI	LI	LI	SC	SC	SC
21	LI	LI	LI	SC	SC	SC	SA
22	LI	LI	SC	SC	SC	SA	SA
23	LI	SC	SC	SC	SA	SA	SA
24	SC	SC	SC	SA	SA	SA	CP
25	SC	SA	SA	SA	CP	CP	CP
26	SA	SA	SA	CP	CP	CP	AQ
27	SA	SA	CP	CP	AQ	AQ	AQ
28	SA	CP	CP	AQ	AQ	AQ	AQ
29	CP	CP	CP	AQ	AQ	AQ	PI

AR = Aries, TA = Taurus, GE = Gemini, CA = Cancer, LE = Leo, VI = Virgo, LI = Libra, SC = Scorpio, SA = Sagittarius, CP = Capricorn, AQ = Aquarius, PI = Pisces

MOON SIGNS

Moon in Aries

You have a strong imagination, courage, determination and a desire to do things in your own way and forge your own path through life.

Originality is a key attribute; you are seldom stuck for ideas although your mind is changeable and you could take the time to focus on individual tasks. Often quick tempered, you take orders from few people and live life at a fast pace. Avoid health problems by taking regular time out for rest and relaxation.

Emotionally, it is important that you talk to those you are closest to and work out your true feelings. Once you discover that people are there to help, there is less necessity for you to do everything yourself.

Moon in Taurus

The Moon in Taurus gives you a courteous and friendly manner, which means you are likely to have many friends.

The good things in life mean a lot to you, as Taurus is an Earth sign that delights in experiences which please the senses. Hence you are probably a lover of good food and drink, which may in turn mean you need to keep an eye on the bathroom scales, especially as looking good is also important to you.

Emotionally you are fairly stable and you stick by your own standards. Taureans do not respond well to change. Intuition also plays an important part in your life.

Moon in Gemini

You have a warm-hearted character, sympathetic and eager to help others. At times reserved, you can also be articulate and chatty: this is part of the paradox of Gemini, which always brings duplicity to the nature. You are interested in current affairs, have a good intellect, and are good company and likely to have many friends. Most of your friends have a high opinion of you and would be ready to defend you should the need arise. However, this is usually unnecessary, as you are quite capable of defending yourself in any verbal confrontation.

Travel is important to your inquisitive mind and you find intellectual stimulus in mixing with people from different cultures. You also gain much from reading, writing and the arts but you do need plenty of rest and relaxation in order to avoid fatigue.

Moon in Cancer

The Moon in Cancer at the time of birth is a fortunate position as Cancer is the Moon's natural home. This means that the qualities of compassion and understanding given by the Moon are especially enhanced in your nature, and you are friendly and sociable and cope well with emotional pressures. You cherish home and family life, and happily do the domestic tasks. Your surroundings are important to you and you hate squalor and filth. You are likely to have a love of music and poetry.

Your basic character, although at times changeable like the Moon itself, depends on symmetry. You aim to make your surroundings comfortable and harmonious, for yourself and those close to you.

Moon in Leo

The best qualities of the Moon and Leo come together to make you warm-hearted, fair, ambitious and self-confident. With good organisational abilities, you invariably rise to a position of responsibility in your chosen career. This is fortunate as you don't enjoy being an 'also-ran' and would rather be an important part of a small organisation than a menial in a large one.

You should be lucky in love, and happy, provided you put in the effort to make a comfortable home for yourself and those close to you. It is likely that you will have a love of pleasure, sport, music and literature. Life brings you many rewards, most of them as a direct result of your own efforts, although you may be luckier than average and ready to make the best of any situation.

Moon in Virgo

You are endowed with good mental abilities and a keen receptive memory, but you are never ostentatious or pretentious. Naturally quite reserved, you still have many friends, especially of the opposite sex. Marital relationships must be discussed carefully and worked at so that they remain harmonious, as personal attachments can be a problem if you do not give them your full attention.

Talented and persevering, you possess artistic qualities and are a good homemaker. Earning your honours through genuine merit, you work long and hard towards your objectives but show little pride in your achievements. Many short journeys will be undertaken in your life.

Moon in Libra

With the Moon in Libra you are naturally popular and make friends easily. People like you, probably more than you realise, you bring fun to a party and are a natural diplomat. For all its good points, Libra is not the most stable of astrological signs and, as a result, your emotions can be a little unstable too. Therefore, although the Moon in Libra is said to be good for love and marriage, your Sun sign and Rising sign will have an important effect on your emotional and loving qualities.

You must remember to relate to others in your decision-making. Co-operation is crucial because Libra represents the 'balance' of life that can only be achieved through harmonious relationships. Conformity is not easy for you because Libra, an Air sign, likes its independence.

Moon in Scorpio

Some people might call you pushy. In fact, all you really want to do is to live life to the full and protect yourself and your family from the pressures of life. Take care to avoid giving the impression of being sarcastic or impulsive and use your energies wisely and constructively.

You have great courage and you invariably achieve your goals by force of personality and sheer effort. You are fond of mystery and are good at predicting the outcome of situations and events. Travel experiences can be beneficial to you.

You may experience problems if you do not take time to examine your motives in a relationship, and also if you allow jealousy, always a feature of Scorpio, to cloud your judgement.

Moon in Sagittarius

The Moon in Sagittarius helps to make you a generous individual with humanitarian qualities and a kind heart. Restlessness may be intrinsic as your mind is seldom still. Perhaps because of this, you have a need for change that could lead you to several major moves during your adult life. You are not afraid to stand your ground when you know your judgement is right, you speak directly and have good intuition.

At work you are quick, efficient and versatile and so you make an ideal employee. You need work to be intellectually demanding and do not enjoy tedious routines.

In relationships, you anger quickly if faced with stupidity or deception, though you are just as quick to forgive and forget. Emotionally, there are times when your heart rules your head.

Moon in Capricorn

The Moon in Capricorn makes you popular and likely to come into the public eye in some way. The watery Moon is not entirely comfortable in the Earth sign of Capricorn and this may lead to some difficulties in the early years of life. An initial lack of creative ability and indecision must be overcome before the true qualities of patience and perseverance inherent in Capricorn can show through.

You have good administrative ability and are a capable worker, and if you are careful you can accumulate wealth. But you must be cautious and take professional advice in partnerships, as you are open to deception. You may be interested in social or welfare work, which suit your organisational skills and sympathy for others.

Moon in Aquarius

The Moon in Aquarius makes you an active and agreeable person with a friendly, easy-going nature. Sympathetic to the needs of others, you flourish in a laid-back atmosphere. You are broad-minded, fair and open to suggestion, although sometimes you have an unconventional quality which others can find hard to understand.

You are interested in the strange and curious, and in old articles and places. You enjoy trips to these places and gain much from them. Political, scientific and educational work interests you and you might choose a career in science or technology.

Money-wise, you make gains through innovation and concentration and Lunar Aquarians often tackle more than one job at a time. In love you are kind and honest.

Moon in Pisces

You have a kind, sympathetic nature, somewhat retiring at times, but you always take account of others' feelings and help when you can.

Personal relationships may be problematic, but as life goes on you can learn from your experiences and develop a better understanding of yourself and the world around you.

You have a fondness for travel, appreciate beauty and harmony and hate disorder and strife. You may be fond of literature and would make a good writer or speaker yourself. You have a creative imagination and may come across as an incurable romantic. You have strong intuition, maybe bordering on a mediumistic quality, which sets you apart from the mass. You may not be rich in cash terms, but your personal gifts are worth more than gold.

AQUARIUS IN LOVE

Discover how compatible in love you are with people from the same and other signs of the zodiac. Five stars equals a match made in heaven!

Aquarius meets Aquarius

This is a good match for several reasons. Most importantly, although it sounds arrogant, Aquarians like themselves. At its best, Aquarius is one of the fairest, most caring and genuinely pleasant zodiac signs and so it is only when faced by the difficulties created by others that it shows a less favourable side. Put two Aquarians together and voilà – instant success! Personal and family life should bring more joy. On the whole, a platform for adventure based on solid foundations. Star rating: *****

Aquarius meets Pisces

Zodiac signs that follow each other often have something in common, but this is not the case with Aquarius and Pisces. Both signs are deeply caring, but in different ways. Pisces is one of the deepest zodiac signs, and Aquarius simply isn't prepared to embark on the journey. Pisceans, meanwhile, would probably find Aquarians superficial and even flippant. On the positive side there is potential for a well-balanced relationship, but unless one party is untypical of their zodiac sign, it often doesn't get started. Star rating: **

Aquarius meets Aries

Aquarius is an Air sign, and Air and Fire often work well together, but not in the case of Aries and Aquarius. The average Aquarian lives in what the Ram sees as a fantasy world, so a meeting of minds is unlikely. Of course, the dominant side of Aries could be trained by the devil-may-care attitude of Aquarius. There are meeting points but they are difficult to establish. However, given sufficient time and an open mind on both sides, a degree of happiness is possible. Star rating: **

Aquarius meets Taurus

In any relationship of which Aquarius is a part, surprises abound. It is difficult for Taurus to understand the soul-searching, adventurous, changeable Aquarian, but on the positive side, the Bull is adaptable and can respond well to a dose of excitement. Aquarians are kind and react well to the same quality coming back at them. Both are friendly, capable of deep affection and basically creative. Unfortunately, Taurus simply doesn't know what makes Aquarius tick, which could lead to feelings of isolation, even if these don't always show on the surface. Star rating: **

Aquarius meets Gemini

Aquarius is commonly mistaken for a Water sign, but in fact it's ruled by the Air element, and this is the key to its compatibility with Gemini. Both signs mix freely socially, and each has an insatiable curiosity. There is plenty of action, lots of love, but very little rest, and so great potential for success if they don't wear each other out! Aquarius revels in its own eccentricity, and encourages Gemini to emulate this. Theirs will be an unconventional household, but almost everyone warms to this crazy and unpredictable couple. Star rating: *****

Aquarius meets Cancer

Cancer is often attracted to Aquarius and, as Aquarius is automatically on the side of anyone who fancies it, so there is the potential for something good here. Cancer loves Aquarius' devil-may-care approach to life, but also recognises and seeks to strengthen the basic lack of self-confidence that all Air signs try so hard to keep secret. Both signs are natural travellers and are quite adventurous. Their family life could be unusual, but friends would recognise a caring, sharing household with many different interests shared by people genuinely in love. Star rating: ***

Aquarius meets Leo

The problem here is that Aquarius doesn't think in the general sense of the word, it knows. Leo, on the other hand, is more practical and relies more on logical reasoning, and consequently it doesn't understand Aquarius very well. Aquarians can also appear slightly frosty in their appreciation of others and this, too, will annoy Leo. This is a good match for a business partnership because Aquarius is astute, while Leo is brave, but personally the prognosis is less promising. Tolerance, understanding and forbearance are all needed to make this work. Star rating: **

Aquarius meets Virgo

Aquarius is a strange sign because no matter how well one knows it, it always manages to surprise. For this reason, against the odds, it's quite likely that Aquarius will form a sucessful relationship with Virgo. Aquarius is changeable, unpredictable and often quite odd, while Virgo is steady, a fuss-pot and very practical. Herein lies the key. What one sign needs, the other provides and that may be the surest recipe for success imaginable. On-lookers may not know why the couple are happy, but they will recognise that this is the case. Star rating: ****

Aquarius meets Libra

One of the best combinations imaginable, partly because both are Air signs and so share a common meeting point. But perhaps the more crucial factor is that both signs respect each other. Aquarius loves life and originality, and is quite intellectual. Libra is similar, but more balanced and rather less eccentric. A visit to this couple's house would be entertaining and full of zany wit, activity and excitement. Both are keen to travel and may prefer to 'find themselves' before taking on too many domestic responsibilities. Star rating: *****

Aquarius meets Scorpio

This is a promising and practical combination. Scorpio responds well to Aquarius' persistent exploration of its deep nature and so this generally shy sign becomes lighter, brighter and more inspirational. Meanwhile, Aquarians are rarely as sure of themselves as they like to appear and are reassured by Scorpio's constant, steady and determined support. Both signs want to be kind to each other, which is a good starting point to a relationship that should be warm most of the time and extremely hot occasionally. Star rating: ****

Aquarius meets Sagittarius

Both Sagittarius and Aquarius are into mind games, which may lead to something of an intellectual competition. If one side is happy to be 'bamboozled' it won't be a problem, but it is more likely that the relationship will turn into a competition, which won't auger well for its long-term future. However, on the plus side, both signs are adventurous and sociable, so as long as there is always something new and interesting to do, the match could turn out very well. Star rating: **

Aquarius meets Capricorn

Probably one of the least likely combinations, as Capricorn and Aquarius are unlikely to choose each other in the first place, unless one side is quite untypical of their sign. Capricorn approaches things in a practical way and likes to get things done, while Aquarius works almost exclusively for the moment and relies heavily on intuition. Their attitudes to romance are also diametrically opposed: Aquarius' moods tend to swing from red hot to ice cold in a minute, which is alien to steady Capricorn. Star rating: **

VENUS: THE PLANET OF LOVE

If you look up at the sky around sunset or sunrise you will often see Venus in close attendance to the Sun. It is arguably one of the most beautiful sights of all and there is little wonder that historically it became associated with the goddess of love. But although Venus does play an important part in the way you view love and in the way others see you romantically, this is only one of the spheres of influence that it enjoys in your overall character.

Venus has a part to play in the more cultured side of your life and has much to do with your appreciation of art, literature, music and general creativity. Even the way you look is responsive to the part of the zodiac that Venus occupied at the start of your life, though this fact is also down to your Sun sign and Ascending sign. If, at the time you were born, Venus occupied one of the more gregarious zodiac signs, you will be more likely to wear your heart on your sleeve, as well as to be more attracted to entertainment, social gatherings and good company. If on the other hand Venus occupied a quiet zodiac sign at the time of your birth, you would tend to be more retiring and less willing to shine in public situations.

It's good to know what part the planet Venus plays in your life for it can have a great bearing on the way you appear to the rest of the world and since we all have to mix with others, you can learn to make the very best of what Venus has to offer you.

One of the great complications in the past has always been trying to establish exactly what zodiac position Venus enjoyed when you were born because the planet is notoriously difficult to track. However, we have solved that problem by creating a table that is exclusive to your Sun sign, which you will find on the following page.

Establishing your Venus sign could not be easier. Just look up the year of your birth on the following page and you will see a sign of the zodiac. This was the sign that Venus occupied in the period covered by your sign in that year. If Venus occupied more than one sign during the period, this is indicated by the date on which the sign changed, and the name of the new sign. For instance, if you were born in 1945, Venus was in Pisces until the 12th February, after which time it was in Aries. If you were born before 12th February your Venus sign is Pisces, if you were born on or after 12th February, your Venus sign is Aries. Once you have established the position of Venus at the time of your birth, you can then look in the pages which follow to see how this has a bearing on your life as a whole.

1915 SAGITTARIUS / 7.2 CAPRICORN
1916 PISCES / 14.2 ARIES
1917 CAPRICORN / 9.2 AQUARIUS
1918 AQUARIUS
1919 AQUARIUS / 3.2 PISCES
1920 SAGITTARIUS / 30.1 CAPRICORN
1921 PISCES / 15.2 ARIES
1922 CAPRICORN / 25.1 AQUARIUS / 18.2 PISCES
1923 SAGITTARIUS / 7.2 CAPRICORN
1924 PISCES / 13.2 ARIES
1925 CAPRICORN / 9.2 AQUARIUS
1926 AQUARIUS
1927 AQUARIUS / 2.2 PISCES
1928 SAGITTARIUS / 29.1 CAPRICORN
1929 PISCES / 14.2 ARIES
1930CAPRICORN / 25.1 AQUARIUS / 18.2 PISCES
1931 SAGITTARIUS / 6.2 CAPRICORN
1932 PISCES / 13.2 ARIES
1933 CAPRICORN / 8.2 AQUARIUS
1934 AQUARIUS
1935 AQUARIUS / 2.2 PISCES
1936 SAGITTARIUS / 29.1 CAPRICORN
1937 PISCES / 13.2 ARIES
1938 CAPRICORN / 24.1 AQUARIUS / 17.2 PISCES
1939 SAGITTARIUS / 6.2 CAPRICORN
1940 PISCES / 12.2 ARIES
1941 CAPRICORN / 8.2 AQUARIUS
1942 AQUARIUS
1943 AQUARIUS / 1.2 PISCES
1944 SAGITTARIUS / 28.1 CAPRICORN
1945 PISCES / 12.2 ARIES
1946 CAPRICORN / 24.1 AQUARIUS / 17.2 PISCES
1947 SAGITTARIUS / 6.2 CAPRICORN
1948 PISCES / 12.2 ARIES
1949 CAPRICORN / 7.2 AQUARIUS
1950 AQUARIUS
1951 AQUARIUS / 1.2 PISCES
1952 SAGITTARIUS / 27.1 CAPRICORN
1953 PISCES / 11.2 ARIES
1954 CAPRICORN / 23.1 AQUARIUS / 16.2 PISCES
1955 SAGITTARIUS / 6.2 CAPRICORN
1956 PISCES / 11.2 ARIES
1957 CAPRICORN / 7.2 AQUARIUS
1958 AQUARIUS
1959 AQUARIUS / 31.1 PISCES
1960 SAGITTARIUS / 27.1 CAPRICORN
1961 PISCES / 9.2 ARIES
1962 CAPRICORN / 23.1 AQUARIUS / 15.2 PISCES
1963 SAGITTARIUS / 6.2 CAPRICORN
1964 PISCES / 11.2 ARIES
1965 CAPRICORN / 6.2 AQUARIUS
1966 AQUARIUS
1967 AQUARIUS / 30.1 PISCES
1968 SAGITTARIUS / 26.1 CAPRICORN
1969 PISCES / 7.2 ARIES
1970 CAPRICORN / 22.1 AQUARIUS / 15.2 PISCES
1971 SAGITTARIUS / 5.2 CAPRICORN
1972 PISCES / 10.2 ARIES
1973 CAPRICORN / 5.2 AQUARIUS
1974 AQUARIUS / 7.2 CAPRICORN
1975 AQUARIUS / 30.1 PISCES
1976 SAGITTARIUS / 26.1 CAPRICORN
1977 PISCES / 5.2 ARIES
1978 CAPRICORN / 22.1 AQUARIUS / 14.2 PISCES
1979 SAGITTARIUS / 5.2 CAPRICORN
1980 PISCES / 10.2 ARIES
1981 CAPRICORN / 5.2 AQUARIUS
1982 AQUARIUS / 29.1 CAPRICORN
1983 AQUARIUS / 29.1 PISCES
1984 SAGITTARIUS / 25.1 CAPRICORN
1985 PISCES / 5.2 ARIES
1986 AQUARIUS / 14.2 PISCES
1987 SAGITTARIUS / 5.2 CAPRICORN
1988 PISCES / 9.2 ARIES
1989 CAPRICORN / 4.2 AQUARIUS
1990 AQUARIUS / 23.1 CAPRICORN
1991 AQUARIUS / 29.1 PISCES
1992 SAGITTARIUS / 25.1 CAPRICORN
1993 PISCES / 4.2 ARIES
1994 AQUARIUS / 13.2 PISCES
1995 SAGITTARIUS / 5.2 CAPRICORN
1996 PISCES / 9.2 ARIES
1997 CAPRICORN / 4.2 AQUARIUS
1998 AQUARIUS / 23.1 CAPRICORN
1999 AQUARIUS / 29.1 PISCES
2000 SAGITTARIUS / 25.1 CAPRICORN
2001 PISCES / 4.2 ARIES
2002 AQUARIUS / 13.2 PISCES
2003 SAGITTARIUS
2004 PISCES / 9.2 AQUARIUS
2005 CAPRICORN / 6.2 AQUARIUS
2006 AQUARIUS / 14.01 CAPRICORN
2007 AQUARIUS / 19.01 PISCES
2008 SAGITTARIUS / 25.1 CAPRICORN
2009 PISCES / 4.2 ARIES
2010 AQUARIUS / 12.2 PISCES
2011 SAGITTARIUS
2012 PISCES / 9.2 AQUARIUS
2013 CAPRICORN / 6.2 AQUARIUS

VENUS THROUGH THE ZODIAC SIGNS

Venus in Aries

Amongst other things, the position of Venus in Aries indicates a fondness for travel, music and all creative pursuits. Your nature tends to be affectionate and you would try not to create confusion or difficulty for others if it could be avoided. Many people with this planetary position have a great love of the theatre, and mental stimulation is of the greatest importance. Early romantic attachments are common with Venus in Aries, so it is very important to establish a genuine sense of romantic continuity. Early marriage is not recommended, especially if it is based on sympathy. You may give your heart a little too readily on occasions.

Venus in Taurus

You are capable of very deep feelings and your emotions tend to last for a very long time. This makes you a trusting partner and lover, whose constancy is second to none. In life you are precise and careful and always try to do things the right way. Although this means an ordered life, which you are comfortable with, it can also lead you to be rather too fussy for your own good. Despite your pleasant nature, you are very fixed in your opinions and quite able to speak your mind. Others are attracted to you and historical astrologers always quoted this position of Venus as being very fortunate in terms of marriage. However, if you find yourself involved in a failed relationship, it could take you a long time to trust again.

Venus in Gemini

As with all associations related to Gemini, you tend to be quite versatile, anxious for change and intelligent in your dealings with the world at large. You may gain money from more than one source but you are equally good at spending it. There is an inference here that you are a good communicator, via either the written or the spoken word, and you love to be in the company of interesting people. Always on the look-out for culture, you may also be very fond of music, and love to indulge the curious and cultured side of your nature. In romance you tend to have more than one relationship and could find yourself associated with someone who has previously been a friend or even a distant relative.

Venus in Cancer

You often stay close to home because you are very fond of family and enjoy many of your most treasured moments when you are with those you love. Being naturally sympathetic, you will always do anything you can to support those around you, even people you hardly know at all. This charitable side of your nature is your most noticeable trait and is one of the reasons why others are naturally so fond of you. Being receptive and in some cases even psychic, you can see through to the soul of most of those with whom you come into contact. You may not commence too many romantic attachments but when you do give your heart, it tends to be unconditionally.

Venus in Leo

It must become quickly obvious to almost anyone you meet that you are kind, sympathetic and yet determined enough to stand up for anyone or anything that is truly important to you. Bright and sunny, you warm the world with your natural enthusiasm and would rarely do anything to hurt those around you, or at least not intentionally. In romance you are ardent and sincere, though some may find your style just a little overpowering. Gains come through your contacts with other people and this could be especially true with regard to romance, for love and money often come hand in hand for those who were born with Venus in Leo. People claim to understand you, though you are more complex than you seem.

Venus in Virgo

Your nature could well be fairly quiet no matter what your Sun sign might be, though this fact often manifests itself as an inner peace and would not prevent you from being basically sociable. Some delays and even the odd disappointment in love cannot be ruled out with this planetary position, though it's a fact that you will usually find the happiness you look for in the end. Catapulting yourself into romantic entanglements that you know to be rather ill-advised is not sensible, and it would be better to wait before you committed yourself exclusively to any one person. It is the essence of your nature to serve the world at large and through doing so it is possible that you will attract money at some stage in your life.

Venus in Libra

Venus is very comfortable in Libra and bestows upon those people who have this planetary position a particular sort of kindness that is easy to recognise. This is a very good position for all sorts of friendships and also for romantic attachments that usually bring much joy into your life. Few individuals with Venus in Libra would avoid marriage and since you are capable of great depths of love, it is likely that you will find a contented personal life. You like to mix with people of integrity and intelligence but don't take kindly to scruffy surroundings or work that means getting your hands too dirty. Careful speculation, good business dealings and money through marriage all seem fairly likely.

Venus in Scorpio

You are quite open and tend to spend money quite freely, even on those occasions when you don't have very much. Although your intentions are always good, there are times when you get yourself in to the odd scrape and this can be particularly true when it comes to romance, which you may come to late or from a rather unexpected direction. Certainly you have the power to be happy and to make others contented on the way, but you find the odd stumbling block on your journey through life and it could seem that you have to work harder than those around you. As a result of this, you gain a much deeper understanding of the true value of personal happiness than many people ever do, and are likely to achieve true contentment in the end.

Venus in Sagittarius

You are lighthearted, cheerful and always able to see the funny side of any situation. These facts enhance your popularity, which is especially high with members of the opposite sex. You should never have to look too far to find romantic interest in your life, though it is just possible that you might be too willing to commit yourself before you are certain that the person in question is right for you. Part of the problem here extends to other areas of life too. The fact is that you like variety in everything and so can tire of situations that fail to offer it. All the same, if you choose wisely and learn to understand your restless side, then great happiness can be yours.

Venus in Capricorn

The most notable trait that comes from Venus in this position is that it makes you trustworthy and able to take on all sorts of responsibilities in life. People are instinctively fond of you and love you all the more because you are always ready to help those who are in any form of need. Social and business popularity can be yours and there is a magnetic quality to your nature that is particularly attractive in a romantic sense. Anyone who wants a partner for a lover, a spouse and a good friend too would almost certainly look in your direction. Constancy is the hallmark of your nature and unfaithfulness would go right against the grain. You might sometimes be a little too trusting.

Venus in Aquarius

This location of Venus offers a fondness for travel and a desire to try out something new at every possible opportunity. You are extremely easy to get along with and tend to have many friends from varied backgrounds, classes and inclinations. You like to live a distinct sort of life and gain a great deal from moving about, both in a career sense and with regard to your home. It is not out of the question that you could form a romantic attachment to someone who comes from far away or be attracted to a person of a distinctly artistic and original nature. What you cannot stand is jealousy, for you have friends of both sexes and would want to keep things that way.

Venus in Pisces

The first thing people tend to notice about you is your wonderful, warm smile. Being very charitable by nature you will do anything to help others, even if you don't know them well. Much of your life may be spent sorting out situations for other people, but it is very important to feel that you are living for yourself too. In the main, you remain cheerful, and tend to be quite attractive to members of the opposite sex. Where romantic attachments are concerned, you could be drawn to people who are significantly older or younger than yourself or to someone with a unique career or point of view. It might be best for you to avoid marrying whilst you are still very young.

AQUARIUS:
2012 DIARY PAGES

October 2012

1 MONDAY *Moon Age Day 15 Moon Sign Aries*

The planetary focus today is on your presently strong personality and the way others view it. Even those you mix with frequently are not always used to seeing the very determined Aquarian, so give them the odd smile or wink to let them know you haven't really changed at all. Nevertheless, remain focused on your objective.

2 TUESDAY *Moon Age Day 16 Moon Sign Taurus*

Though there is little doubt your ego is strong at the moment, you retain your usual ability to turn on the charm when necessary. This is fortunate because you need to let those around you know how much you care about them and also reassure family members of your continued practical and emotional support.

3 WEDNESDAY *Moon Age Day 17 Moon Sign Taurus*

What really sets you apart right now is your ability to speak in public situations, and to elicit the necessary response from others. This is nothing particularly new but is a quality much enhanced by present planetary trends. In a business sense, it is possible that new ideas are coming along at all stages today.

4 THURSDAY *Moon Age Day 18 Moon Sign Taurus*

You are ready for almost any challenge life can throw at you, plus a few you invent for yourself. All the same, you don't have to go to extremes just to get some excitement into your life. If you haven't enough to do, there are people nearby who would welcome a helping hand.

5 FRIDAY *Moon Age Day 19 Moon Sign Gemini*

In money matters, your present ability to think quickly is going to prove extremely useful. Although you are unlikely to be gambling in the generally accepted sense of the word, it might be worth taking a chance that could lead to greater monetary strength further down the line. Make time to enjoy yourself later in the day.

6 SATURDAY *Moon Age Day 20 Moon Sign Gemini*

You should be feeling quietly confident, particularly when you are dealing with familiar subjects. Your creative potential is especially strong and shows itself through all facets of life. There may not be time to do everything you have planned today, but you will be determined to have a really good try.

7 SUNDAY *Moon Age Day 21 Moon Sign Cancer*

Not everyone you know proves to be adept at expressing either their opinions or wishes today. This leads to a good deal of second-guessing as far as you are concerned. The challenge today is to keep one step ahead of the competition. This is as true if you happen to be at work as it is in social or sporting situations.

8 MONDAY *Moon Age Day 22 Moon Sign Cancer*

Your wits are sharp and effective so make sure you are getting your message across clearly – it shouldn't be a problem. Of course, you can't expect to see eye to eye with everyone, and especially not at a time when you are quite assertive. All the same, try to keep disagreements to a minimum.

9 TUESDAY *Moon Age Day 23 Moon Sign Cancer*

Don't be fooled into making any purchase that you know is flippant or unnecessary. Keep a cool head in a minor crisis and you will soon be laughing at the whole situation. Financial consolidation is on your mind and you could be looking at family money very closely indeed.

10 WEDNESDAY *Moon Age Day 24 Moon Sign Leo*

Not all plans are working out strictly as you might have wished today and there is a good deal of thinking on your feet to be done. The way other people are behaving can give you food for thought, but since you are extremely intuitive at present, you should be able to work out their reasoning.

11 THURSDAY *Moon Age Day 25 Moon Sign Leo*

If you are finding that you are not as efficient as usual, it's all the more reason to allow colleagues and friends to take some of the strain. There could be some slightly uncomfortable moments in situations relating to love, maybe as a result of your inability to say or do the right thing. It might be best to do nothing at all.

12 FRIDAY *Moon Age Day 26 Moon Sign Virgo*

With the lunar low now well out of the way, your ability to get on with others at a fundamental level is well accented. Don't worry if you can't do every job quite as quickly and efficiently as you might wish, because most of them will be fine. Domestic and personal relationships turn out to be the best sphere in which to concentrate your efforts today.

13 SATURDAY *Moon Age Day 27 Moon Sign Virgo*

Long-term planning can be thwarted by the contrary opinions of family members and some extra latitude is necessary when dealing with people who feel they have an axe to grind. Confidence isn't exactly brimming over today but that does not have to prevent you from making a good deal of progress in minor issues.

14 SUNDAY *Moon Age Day 28 Moon Sign Libra*

Current planetary trends seem to be bringing out the home-bird in you. This is slightly unusual for Aquarius and tends to hold you back somewhat in a practical and professional sense. This is a temporary trend so don't let it worry you unduly.

15 MONDAY *Moon Age Day 0 Moon Sign Libra*

This may be a day to go travelling and you would certainly enjoy the thrill of any chase that has a social aspect. Romance should also be highlighted, though these trends turn inwards, towards those individuals you already know and perhaps towards an old flame that might be starting to burn brightly again.

16 TUESDAY *Moon Age Day 1 Moon Sign Libra*

Your main area of fulfilment today brings you back, once again, towards home and family. You can succeed in facing life's challenges, but only by seeking the help and advice of those you love. You can see your way forward marked clearly, but can you make the wholesale changes that you instinctively know will be necessary?

17 WEDNESDAY *Moon Age Day 2 Moon Sign Scorpio*

A fair and dispassionate view of life is called for, without any obstacles created by past prejudices. You need to be open and fair, even with those who have not always given you the benefit of the doubt. Beware of some emotional drives that could force you to make decisions that would not help your cause at all.

18 THURSDAY *Moon Age Day 3 Moon Sign Scorpio*

Now you have the chance to shine more and to show superiors what you are capable of doing. Work plays a much more important part in your life at this stage of the month so don't neglect it. At the same time, your concern for home and family is undiminished.

19 FRIDAY *Moon Age Day 4 Moon Sign Sagittarius*

The lunar high this month should bring some excitement, plus a chance to follow your own will to a greater extent. Your powers of communication appear to be accented, so if you need to impress anyone, now is the time to go out and do it.

20 SATURDAY *Moon Age Day 5 Moon Sign Sagittarius*

Being around new faces can lift your spirits no end. Make sure that's what you are doing because you'll gain nothing by spending time thinking about the past or mixing with people who are a drain on your emotions. The greater your confidence and sense of self-worth, the better you will do in a material sense.

21 SUNDAY *Moon Age Day 6 Moon Sign Capricorn*

You might have to put up with second best in one or two situations today but your ability to plan for the future has rarely been better. Give yourself credit for a certain series of successes in personal matters. Don't insist on everything running absolutely smoothly because this is not likely to be the case today.

22 MONDAY *Moon Age Day 7 Moon Sign Capricorn*

Immediately ahead of the lunar high, the Moon in your solar twelfth house offers a time to pause and to assess what is going on around you. It is possible that you fail to make any progress at all today, but then, if you are sensible, you are not really trying to do so. Tomorrow is the time for action.

23 TUESDAY *Moon Age Day 8 Moon Sign Aquarius*

Personal gambles pay off now, even though too much speculation is not really your forte. When it comes to reaching an almost perfect understanding in a romantic sense, you are second to none, and making almost everyone you come across feel comfortable is also easy to achieve.

24 WEDNESDAY *Moon Age Day 9 Moon Sign Aquarius*

This is a day for excitement and almost certainly not a time you would want to spend relaxing with your feet up. You should be aiming to contribute very positively to your own future a fact that is obvious to you. Results from very real effort you have been putting in of late now begin to make themselves felt.

25 THURSDAY *Moon Age Day 10 Moon Sign Pisces*

It may be necessary to rearrange your schedules somewhat, possibly to accommodate others. Putting yourself out in this way has hidden benefits. You continue to be fond of the good things in life and there isn't much doubt that luxury in one form or another is going to play an important part around this time.

26 FRIDAY *Moon Age Day 11 Moon Sign Pisces*

Beware of having a slight prima donna approach to some situations. This will only occur in matters about which you know a great deal and where others are trying to muscle in on you. All the same, yours is the most conciliatory of natures and this state of affairs should not change today.

27 SATURDAY *Moon Age Day 12 Moon Sign Aries*

Finding the time to let your partner know how important they are to you would be ideal today. Those Aquarians looking for love should turn up the light of their passion. Material affairs are slightly less stable today, which is why you could be deferring decisions and turning your mind towards personal matters instead.

28 SUNDAY *Moon Age Day 13 Moon Sign Aries*

It looks as though you are gradually achieving your chosen objectives, even though the going might have been tougher than you would have thought. Aquarians who have been slimming or trying to get fitter should now begin to realise that progress is being made, whilst those looking for changes at home can find them.

29 MONDAY *Moon Age Day 14 Moon Sign Aries*

People who don't often figure in your life might put in guest appearances and it is not out of the question that you could meet someone who has been something of an idol in the past. You can easily express your ideas at the moment and that's what counts if you want to get on in most situations.

30 TUESDAY *Moon Age Day 15 Moon Sign Taurus*

Avoid looking back too much today because it won't really help at the moment. You should be pretty much in tune with your financial goals and general objectives and since you spend quite a lot of your time worrying about money, this should turn out to be a very positive state of affairs.

31 WEDNESDAY *Moon Age Day 16 Moon Sign Taurus*

Planetary influences of a very positive nature are around now and the best focus of all is on finances, so you should be concentrating on attracting greater resources. Don't waste the positive opportunities that life is holding out to you and use your intuition to recognise them.

November

2012

1 THURSDAY *Moon Age Day 17 Moon Sign Gemini*

You would do well to apply yourself to some creative enterprise and should enjoy the challenge this represents. What is certain is that you are starting to go through a fairly hectic phase and one that precludes much rest. However, you have what it takes to deal with greater social demands.

2 FRIDAY *Moon Age Day 18 Moon Sign Gemini*

Routines can seem to be a real bind and there will always be something more interesting in prospect. That's the way the Aquarian mind works sometimes. In one way or another you need to find change and diversity and would not take kindly be being tied down to the same place all day.

3 SATURDAY *Moon Age Day 19 Moon Sign Gemini*

This ought to be a more relaxed sort of day and one during which you can take your time. This is in direct contrast to some of the profound recent trends. Spending some hours with family members will probably seem quite attractive as will reading or simply watching television.

4 SUNDAY *Moon Age Day 20 Moon Sign Cancer*

Concentration is a keyword at present and remains so until the middle of next week. Your mental processes are working well and other people should pay you plenty of attention. Better financial propositions are coming your way but you need to be sure that you are attentive enough to recognise them when they do.

5 MONDAY *Moon Age Day 21 Moon Sign Cancer*

You can't get everything you want today in a material sense but it is clear that the things in life that are most important to you at present have little or nothing to do with money. In social situations, you can prove to be lively and good company so you should be getting plenty of invitations. If not, hand some out yourself.

6 TUESDAY *Moon Age Day 22 Moon Sign Leo*

Expect a brief lull in proceedings whilst the Moon passes through your opposite zodiac sign of Leo. You might have to accept second best in a situation relating to a loved one and your ability to get exactly what you want from life is not quite as well tuned now as it has been for the last few days.

7 WEDNESDAY ☿ *Moon Age Day 23 Moon Sign Leo*

If you experience some personal set-backs, try not to let them worry you. Don't get involved in too many new ventures and show yourself willing to listen to the sound advice other people offer. The lunar low is somewhat watered down this month by the support you find developing on all sides.

8 THURSDAY ☿ *Moon Age Day 24 Moon Sign Leo*

Everyday concerns seem somehow amplified but it is really only your mood that matters. This would not be the best time to tempt fate by embarking on risky ventures. The path to progress is fairly rocky, so avoid the pitfalls by staying put and waiting for a better time to branch out.

9 FRIDAY ☿ *Moon Age Day 25 Moon Sign Virgo*

This would be a good time to start looking for a new job or thinking in terms of taking on different responsibilities. Stay around influential people, as they are likely to be looking on you very kindly. They could even offer you new opportunities; certainly they will be brightening things up no end at work.

10 SATURDAY ☿ *Moon Age Day 26 Moon Sign Virgo*

A spirit of equality predominates today, which makes it easy for you to associate with just about anyone. Even if you find yourself in settings where you don't usually fit it, you'll be able to relax and enjoy the company of people with different backgrounds or interests.

11 SUNDAY ☿ *Moon Age Day 27 Moon Sign Libra*

Although those around you might prove to be rather cautious in their approach to life, this cannot be said to be true of you. Reconciling your own needs with those of family members might prove difficult at times. The atmosphere in social settings is very good and a generally lively Aquarian is clearly on display.

12 MONDAY ☿ *Moon Age Day 28 Moon Sign Libra*

Most career initiatives are now going well but there are areas of life that prove to be significantly less fulfilling. Some confusion could arise if you fail to say exactly what you mean at work, whilst associates are less than willing to take the sort of chances that come as second nature to you.

13 TUESDAY ☿ *Moon Age Day 0 Moon Sign Scorpio*

Your view of life is sensible and you are also showing an unaccustomed humility that everyone respects. In social settings your silver tongue really helps. Negotiations of almost any sort now work out well and there will be few less auspicious days than this for getting together with colleagues.

14 WEDNESDAY ☿ *Moon Age Day 1 Moon Sign Scorpio*

The atmosphere at work looks as though it will be harmonious and you are not likely to have too many problems today. You need to be sure of yourself before embarking on new projects about which you know nothing and it might be sensible to ask someone who knows better than you do.

15 THURSDAY ☿ *Moon Age Day 2 Moon Sign Sagittarius*

You should still be filled with energy and very keen to get on with things. The only slight problem could be that others are not. You will constantly have to prod people to get what you want and that might be slightly irritating. Money matters look reasonably good and you might be better off than you thought.

16 FRIDAY ☿ *Moon Age Day 3 Moon Sign Sagittarius*

Where major decisions are concerned, you should weigh up the pros and cons carefully, which could lead to some delays. Family parties are possible and if so you will want to do some of the organising. There's just a slight tendency for you to dither today – maybe you've caught the habit from everyone else.

17 SATURDAY ☿ *Moon Age Day 4 Moon Sign Capricorn*

You may seem to be struggling against a tide of negativity coming from those around you but unfortunately there's not much you can do but ride it out. Don't let it bother you because it won't have much impact. Watch out for emotional high points in both your love life and social and leisure activities.

18 SUNDAY ☿ *Moon Age Day 5 Moon Sign Capricorn*

Now the Moon tends to hinder you as it moves into your solar twelfth house. This makes you rather more introspective and even emotional than has been the case for the last few days and it is certain to slow you down somewhat. Even if you have specific objectives, it's not really worth trying too hard today.

19 MONDAY ☿ *Moon Age Day 6 Moon Sign Aquarius*

Even if it appears that you have a mountain of work in front of you, if you apply your concentration it won't take long to get it sorted and then you can begin enjoying yourself. With renewed self-belief and energy, you should attack and deal with any obstacles today.

20 TUESDAY ☿ *Moon Age Day 7 Moon Sign Aquarius*

Don't just settle for too little but go out to get what you really want from life. You are progressive, positive and very cheerful. All practical issues can be addressed now in the almost certain knowledge that you are able to succeed. This is the time of the month during which progress is most likely.

21 WEDNESDAY ☿ *Moon Age Day 8 Moon Sign Pisces*

You will want to do everything you can today to improve circumstances at work and to rationalise jobs that you consider are taking far too long. This is when you are at your happiest and you can score significant successes with colleagues and bosses. Socially speaking you could be in for a slightly quieter period.

22 THURSDAY ☿ *Moon Age Day 9 Moon Sign Pisces*

Work matters and the general headway you are making is well accentuated but there are slight stumbling blocks to be dealt with on the way. Despite this you can still make significant progress and won't be held back, even when those closest to you seem to be running on half speed.

23 FRIDAY ☿ *Moon Age Day 10 Moon Sign Pisces*

Although you may think acting on impulse might prove problematic, in fact it will be the best way to solve any slight difficulties as and when they arise. Avoid games of chance today but do look out for the chance of new relationships. These won't necessarily be romantic but should prove fortunate.

24 SATURDAY ☿ *Moon Age Day 11 Moon Sign Aries*

Although you may find it hard to get ahead in practical ways, you should focus on arranging new strategies and should have time to think things through. Friendly co-operation is what counts now. Work hard, then you should have time for some genuine relaxation.

25 SUNDAY ☿ *Moon Age Day 12 Moon Sign Aries*

Joint finances are worth a second look now and you will most likely be quite happy to spend a few hours sorting out such things. You won't mind because there are strong family trends around today and a genuine need to be in the company of your partner or other family members.

26 MONDAY ☿ *Moon Age Day 13 Moon Sign Taurus*

What you won't be able to stand at the moment is being told what to do by people who have no real idea about you, your life or, more importantly, your capabilities. You are now fairly secure regarding your feelings about yourself. As a result you will argue your corner very well and with much justification.

27 TUESDAY ☿ *Moon Age Day 14 Moon Sign Taurus*

The sheer amount of effort you are prepared to put in to something you really want is almost monumental and even surpasses the Aquarian's usual staying power. This would be a good day to be working on a major time-consuming project. You have plenty of patience and enough resilience to see things through.

28 WEDNESDAY *Moon Age Day 15 Moon Sign Taurus*

Don't be shy when it comes to examining every nook and cranny of any circumstance to find what you want. Aquarius can be very nosey and today you are allowed to give free reign to that quality. There are some indications of success on the way, even if you have to peek under the bedclothes of life to see them.

29 THURSDAY *Moon Age Day 16 Moon Sign Gemini*

Beware because there could be some slight conflict today. It will probably be with colleagues if you are at work or maybe with a friend if you are not. Gains can come through family members and might also be evident if you take the trouble to rummage through the attic to find what someone thinks is a treasure.

30 FRIDAY *Moon Age Day 17 Moon Sign Gemini*

There are many situations that are beyond your own control and none of them is worth a moment of concern. Your imagination could be working overtime today and that's a mixed blessing. If you are planning for the future, that's great but there is always the possibility you will be inventing things to worry about.

December 2012

1 SATURDAY *Moon Age Day 18 Moon Sign Cancer*

Work and all practical matters receive a definite boost now and it isn't hard for you to get what you want in a material sense. Don't be too quick to believe everything you hear, especially where your personal or family life is concerned. If you have to sign documents, read the small print.

2 SUNDAY *Moon Age Day 19 Moon Sign Cancer*

You could be dealing in nostalgia at the moment, which although fairly understandable at this time of year, isn't really worth much in practice. All the same, there are different spheres of your life and as long as your desire to get ahead doesn't get dented, it's okay to look back.

3 MONDAY *Moon Age Day 20 Moon Sign Cancer*

Your communication skills are now second to none and you won't have any problem making the sort of impression that ensures you are high on everyone's Christmas list. You can bring out the best in others now and it ought to be obvious from the moment you get out of bed that you want to get on with things in a positive way.

4 TUESDAY *Moon Age Day 21 Moon Sign Leo*

The lunar low is not likely to be particularly noticeable this month, though it might simply tend to slow down the progress you feel you have been making over the last few days. Keep a check on spending until later in the week, if possible. Keep major plans and appointments on the backburner for now.

5 WEDNESDAY *Moon Age Day 22 Moon Sign Leo*

You may not want to travel very far and if you find yourself off on a shopping spree, make sure you are not in the company of people who frustrate you. You should be putting off doing anything that isn't really important and spend part of the day lounging in luxury or simply with those close to you.

6 THURSDAY *Moon Age Day 23 Moon Sign Virgo*

It seems as though you need to feel quite secure and the little luxuries of life enhance that security. All thoughts of planning for Christmas could be out of the window for now. Although your hearth and home may continue to be your main source of interest, you are likely to be going through a rather indulgent phase.

7 FRIDAY *Moon Age Day 24 Moon Sign Virgo*

You now have enough energy and sufficient determination to ensure that you win through in the end. In pursuit of your major ideals and objectives today, you might encounter one or two stumbling blocks. Don't allow these to hold you back because there is no reason for them to do so.

8 SATURDAY *Moon Age Day 25 Moon Sign Libra*

It seems as though a little soul-searching might be in order at the start of this weekend. It is possible you took certain actions last week that you now wish you had not. It might be impossible to redress the situation but there are ways you can explain yourself. The evening should be good for romantic proposals.

9 SUNDAY *Moon Age Day 26 Moon Sign Libra*

You have it within your nature to make others extremely happy and won't be likely to show jealousy in personal attachments, even if you are being pushed in some way. This is a particularly good time for entertaining at home and for dealing with those little details that make all the difference.

10 MONDAY *Moon Age Day 27 Moon Sign Scorpio*

Professional matters are definitely looking better and more successful by the minute, even if this situation may be brought to a temporary halt by the arrival of some slight stumbling blocks. It may be around this time that you first get your Christmas head on. Shopping, by yourself or with friends, might be inevitable.

11 TUESDAY *Moon Age Day 28 Moon Sign Scorpio*

This is a marvellous period for twosomes and a time when you will be happiest in the arms of your lover. Present planetary positions make it possible for you to express yourself fully and there are likely to be some incredible compliments coming your way. Do an extra bit of work today in order to save time later.

12 WEDNESDAY *Moon Age Day 0 Moon Sign Sagittarius*

You should be well aware of the people who can do you the greatest favours at this stage of the month and you would be rather foolish to turn away their kindness. In terms of your career, you should be looking impressive now and the same is true if you are presently involved in any form of education.

13 THURSDAY *Moon Age Day 1 Moon Sign Sagittarius*

There is room to change your mind at work but less flexibility in home-based matters. People tend to be quite demanding and you will need to be in three places at once. Close ties may not bring out the best in you right now and you would be better off spending time with casual friends.

14 FRIDAY *Moon Age Day 2 Moon Sign Capricorn*

The approach of the weekend could bring a slight reversal in fortunes but any disappointments are likely to be short-lived. Not everything goes quite as well as you would wish but you remain generally cheerful. Support is available where finances are concerned, even if this is only in an advisory sense.

15 SATURDAY *Moon Age Day 3 Moon Sign Capricorn*

Keep major plans and appointments to a minimum and clear the decks for action later. The Moon is in your solar twelfth house, probably putting you in the most nostalgic mood of the month. There's nothing wrong with enjoying the emotional side of December, which is what you might be doing now.

16 SUNDAY *Moon Age Day 4 Moon Sign Aquarius*

Your health and vitality are both likely to be excellent so today you should show a warm, understanding but still very progressive face to the world. First to join in any silly games, you really should be the life and soul of the pre-Christmas party scene – which is likely to be an enduring theme for you this year.

17 MONDAY *Moon Age Day 5 Moon Sign Aquarius*

Plans that are presently on the boil get an extra boost and there is no stopping you on your personal quest to make the sort of splash that is bound to get you noticed. There are quite a few people around whose sole desire in life seems to be to support you. Take opportunities as and when they arise.

18 TUESDAY *Moon Age Day 6 Moon Sign Aquarius*

You now have the chance to get ahead in something that is quite important to you so grab it and tell people what you think about the situation. In a financial sense, this is a time of short-term increase, so you may as well enjoy the gains while they last. Not that cash is likely to stay with you for long at this time of year.

19 WEDNESDAY *Moon Age Day 7 Moon Sign Pisces*

If the approach of Christmas becomes a bore, then most of the happiness surrounding it disappears altogether, so make it interesting. Don't be embarrassed to be as excited as a child. Everyday life should be fairly smooth now and there will be plenty of time for enjoyment, which is what is needed at this time of year.

20 THURSDAY *Moon Age Day 8 Moon Sign Pisces*

Although you can still be making gains at work, the actions or ideas of colleagues could be taking the shine off the proceedings. Get work out of the way, then you will be able to relax. It is the domestic arena that offers the best chance of interesting developments and happiness today.

21 FRIDAY *Moon Age Day 9 Moon Sign Aries*

It is likely that you will be slightly more judgemental today than usual for your zodiac sign. Whether this turns out to be a good thing or not really depends on the evidence you have to hand. Perhaps it would be better if you started expecting people to help rather than to hinder you.

22 SATURDAY *Moon Age Day 10 Moon Sign Aries*

You probably won't want to spend much time alone today. On the contrary, the more the merrier seems to be your adage at present, so make sure you are in company as much as possible. Look around for some intelligent and interesting conversations today because you can gain a great deal from them.

23 SUNDAY *Moon Age Day 11 Moon Sign Taurus*

Although things are still going generally the way you might wish, not everyone is quite as happy as you are. Once you realise this, you will probably want to do something to help. Ask the right questions and you should find that you can offer some simple but effective solutions.

24 MONDAY *Moon Age Day 12 Moon Sign Taurus*

Your mind is filled with a combination of excitement and nostalgia, which is fairly typical for you on this day. Creative pursuits suit you fine on this particular Christmas Eve so perhaps you are finishing off those last shiny angels for the tree or making an extra special job of wrapping the presents.

25 TUESDAY *Moon Age Day 13 Moon Sign Taurus*

Although you can really have fun, it is just possible that you will feel restless, which is why you need to be on the move. This ought to be a particularly enjoyable Christmas Day in almost every respect. Don't be surprised if you have the urge to travel somewhere, perhaps to see relatives or friends.

26 WEDNESDAY *Moon Age Day 14 Moon Sign Gemini*

Aquarius will feel self-indulgent and extravagant today, which is fine as long as you accept this and keep yourself under control to some extent. The attitude of people you thought you knew well could be surprising and it is possible that you will be called upon to show significant patience.

27 THURSDAY *Moon Age Day 15 Moon Sign Gemini*

Not everyone is going to be in tune with your ideas but that doesn't matter too much at present. There should be plenty of opportunity to talk to your life-partner today and to do so could find you reaching a newer and better understanding of particular situations.

28 FRIDAY *Moon Age Day 16 Moon Sign Cancer*

In personal attachments, avoid the little green-eyed monster of jealousy because if you don't you could look somewhat foolish. This could turn out to be one of the best days of the month to be out and about.

29 SATURDAY *Moon Age Day 17 Moon Sign Cancer*

Although you have been quite busy over Christmas, you can afford to relax a little now and to receive some of the accolades that are rightfully yours. Energy levels remain essentially high.

30 SUNDAY *Moon Age Day 18 Moon Sign Cancer*

There is now a slight tendency to feel trapped, which is something you should fight against as hard as you can. The burning need for freedom is once again at the forefront of your mind.

31 MONDAY *Moon Age Day 19 Moon Sign Leo*

Maybe you are hosting a New Year party or are particularly taken up with the needs of your family. Either way, you are good in an organisational sense and may use your instincts to ensure everyone is happy. Try to relax a little though because the lunar low is around at this time.

AQUARIUS: 2013 DIARY PAGES

AQUARIUS: YOUR YEAR IN BRIEF

People born under the astrological sign of Aquarius love to be perpetually on the go, so you will be happy to learn that this should be possible almost from the very start of the year. Get yourself into the right position to make advancements at work and do all you can to elevate yourself in the minds of bosses and superiors. These trends, though altering in their focus from day to day, perpetuate throughout most of January and February, and offer you a chance to really shine.

The approach of the spring in March and April finds you on top form and still keen to get ahead whenever circumstances allow. However, you might now be keener to address matters of the heart and to give extra attention to family and friends. Any money that comes your way now is likely to be as much as a result of luck as good planning on your part.

The year moves on. May and June should see you making adequate progress and you might even be able to achieve a longed-for objective, maybe something to do with travel. There is a greater likelihood of financial gains and a better sense of purpose at work, with more in the way of personal satisfaction. These trends continue during June but around this time you need to be careful not to promote your own interests at the expense of those of others.

The warmer the weather gets, the happier you should be, and this is especially the case during July, which could turn out to be the happiest and most contented month of the year for you. Both July and August offer you the chance to travel, and since all opportunities to see new places please Aquarius no end, you should be in your element. Don't be too critical of others at this time and be willing to accept a different point of view when it is offered to you.

It is during September and October that you may come to realise just how capable you can be. During both these months you have scope to discover skills you didn't know you possessed, and can certainly impress other people with your abilities. Personal attachments mean more to you than ever at this stage of the year, and some Aquarius people could be finding new love under October's autumn star.

Have confidence in yourself at the very end of the year and trust to your innate sense of what will work out well. Romance is definitely more highlighted at this time than at any other period during the year, and you should be energetic and progressive during both November and December. Christmas should offer you a great deal more than you expect, both in terms of surprises and upward turns in relationships.

January

2013

1 TUESDAY *Moon Age Day 19 Moon Sign Leo*

It may be difficult to exert your desired level of influence over others at this time. If there is a journey that needs to be made, it's worth getting the details sorted out well in advance, and you may also need to be prepared to make alterations to your life at a basic level. Most importantly of all, don't fall out with people you rely on!

2 WEDNESDAY *Moon Age Day 20 Moon Sign Virgo*

This has potential to be a very light-hearted sort of day, filled with promise and the chance to make the very best sort of impression, particularly in a professional sense. You may find yourself somewhat restricted by the demands others are making of you, but reorganising your schedule to compensate shouldn't be too difficult.

3 THURSDAY *Moon Age Day 21 Moon Sign Virgo*

Domestic matters offer a sense of release and can prevent you from feeling that life is all stress and push. Actually there's nothing wrong with stepping out of the rat race now and choosing instead to have fun. This can be found with your family, or friends who are also anxious to enjoy themselves.

4 FRIDAY *Moon Age Day 22 Moon Sign Virgo*

Be ready to react to the twists and turns of your life, particularly away from work. Most of these should be positive in nature and give you an excellent opportunity to impress the world at large. Creative potential is well accented, assisting you to focus on changes you want to make in and around your home.

5 SATURDAY *Moon Age Day 23 Moon Sign Libra*

Dealing decisively with past situations should now help you to feel slightly more positive about your personal life and the way it is going. This is an ideal interlude for beginning new regimes, so what better time to look carefully at what you are eating and how fit you are, well ahead of the spring.

6 SUNDAY *Moon Age Day 24 Moon Sign Libra*

Decision making may not be easy today. There are signs that your judgement may be slightly impaired, and you need to ensure that you keep things in perspective when discussing matters with family, friends and colleagues alike. There could be a few moments today when you wish you had stayed in bed!

7 MONDAY *Moon Age Day 25 Moon Sign Scorpio*

The spotlight is now on the personal impact you can have on others. Keep abreast of things that are happening in and around your home at the moment because you can clearly benefit from some of them. Be willing to seek help from friends, and to make good use of the valuable information they impart.

8 TUESDAY *Moon Age Day 26 Moon Sign Scorpio*

This is not a time to allow yourself to become bored with routines or conventions for which you can see no point whatsoever. It's clear that there is plenty to be done, and there are gains to be made if you get cracking as early in the day as you can manage. Finding time to call your own might not be very easy.

9 WEDNESDAY *Moon Age Day 27 Moon Sign Sagittarius*

Career matters are in a very progressive state, despite the fact that a few minor trends today might stop you in your tracks in this regard. Don't worry, you can still look and plan ahead. This shouldn't prevent you from finding something personally interesting to do with your day. Perhaps a shopping trip might be fun.

10 THURSDAY *Moon Age Day 28 Moon Sign Sagittarius*

Today you find yourself among influences that assist you to keep in touch with the world at large. There are significant gains to be made if you give matters your full attention, particularly in a professional setting. Confidence shouldn't be hard to find, though it does depend on whether or not you feel you are being fully appreciated.

11 FRIDAY *Moon Age Day 29 Moon Sign Capricorn*

So long as you don't take yourself, or anyone else for that matter, too much for granted, you can make things go reasonably well at this time. You can afford to be in the mood to compromise, which pleases colleagues and friends. At home you need to look for words of affection that are on offer before long.

12 SATURDAY *Moon Age Day 0 Moon Sign Capricorn*

The idealistic side of your nature is highlighted at the moment, suggesting that you won't settle for anything less than what you know is fair and just. That's fine, but it won't help if you cut off your nose to spite your face. There are many ways of going about doing things, and it pays to consider this before opening your mouth.

13 SUNDAY *Moon Age Day 1 Moon Sign Aquarius*

Today works best if you remain in a good mood and show that you are prepared to have a go at almost anything. The ambitious qualities within your nature are presently very strong, leading to a willingness to take a chance. The lunar high is around, offering plenty of scope to tap into some favourable luck.

14 MONDAY *Moon Age Day 2 Moon Sign Aquarius*

New ventures are par for the course, particularly if you demonstrate an adventurous and physical approach to life. Almost anything that is on offer is grist to the mill of both your curiosity and your determination. It's time to use your social skills and your disarming manner to get yourself to the top of the popularity stakes.

15 TUESDAY *Moon Age Day 3 Moon Sign Pisces*

In a social sense your winning ways can make all the difference now, and can help you to get what you want from other people. Turn on the charm and see how easily you can persuade everyone round to your point of view. Even if the weather outside isn't very good at present, a little fresh air would do you no harm at all.

16 WEDNESDAY *Moon Age Day 4 Moon Sign Pisces*

Talking to others is the name of the game today, and you needn't fight shy of saying what you think. Be prepared to display the true originality of your zodiac sign and to feel fairly confident in most of your decisions. If you don't know what you are doing, there is much to be said for seeking some help.

17 THURSDAY *Moon Age Day 5 Moon Sign Aries*

Relying on others is all very well, though if necessary you should be ready to plough ahead on your own and make it plain that you won't be held up. It's good to get positive reactions, but if this isn't possible you have the ability to talk your way through situations under present planetary trends.

18 FRIDAY *Moon Age Day 6 Moon Sign Aries*

Today offers you the chance to put yourself fairly and squarely in the limelight. The only real requirement is that you understand fully what is being expected of you. If you are unsure, make certain that you get on top of the situation before you are put to the test in a very public way.

19 SATURDAY *Moon Age Day 7 Moon Sign Aries*

You might have to deal with some unusual situations today, leading to a feeling that your mind is somewhat more muddled than has been the case of late. Sometimes it's necessary to recognise that you are out of your depth or unable to break through the entrenched ideas that others are displaying at present.

20 SUNDAY *Moon Age Day 8 Moon Sign Taurus*

It's a well-known fact that Aquarius, like all the Air signs, has a tendency to run pretty much on its nerves. Even if you give the impression of being bomb-proof, nothing could be further from the truth. The trick is to put on a very confident face, even in situations that have you quaking in your shoes.

21 MONDAY *Moon Age Day 9 Moon Sign Taurus*

Activity of any sort is what today is all about. Most Aquarians have potential to be firing on all cylinders, though you shouldn't run away with the idea that you can push yourself to the absolute limit. You need rest, like everyone else, and should consider whether you are really getting enough at the moment.

22 TUESDAY *Moon Age Day 10 Moon Sign Gemini*

An ideal day to explore new possibilities, and maybe one that involves some sort of business partnership. You don't necessarily need to do much about this right now, but you can at least put plans into action and talk to the right people. Don't be tardy when it comes to offering any congratulations that are due in the family.

23 WEDNESDAY *Moon Age Day 11 Moon Sign Gemini*

Start new projects as you mean to go on, especially those associated with house and home. You have what it takes to persuade others to help you, so this is a favourable time to get things done. Your capacity for keeping going is emphasised, though it might be difficult to find excitement in social and romantic spheres.

24 THURSDAY *Moon Age Day 12 Moon Sign Gemini*

You can't afford to give anyone the impression you are wavering today. The adage 'give an inch and people will take a mile' seems to be very appropriate. Present trends encourage you to stick to your original views in a number of matters. If this makes you stubborn, at least it might also convince people to toe the line.

25 FRIDAY *Moon Age Day 13 Moon Sign Cancer*

However much you need to do today, you are able to commit yourself to whatever is at hand and work through it steadily. As the weekend approaches, you might decide to spend at least some time relaxing. Mixing freely with friends you find to be particularly amusing should be a natural aspect of life now.

26 SATURDAY *Moon Age Day 14 Moon Sign Cancer*

It's worth keeping a sense of proportion regarding any situations that seem to be running out of control. This is not a time to panic about anything, and you can do yourself a great deal of good by simply playing it cool. If you're seeking fame or even notoriety, you could do worse than pursue it now.

27 SUNDAY *Moon Age Day 15 Moon Sign Leo*

The lull represented by the lunar low may be difficult to deal with. Why not settle for a stay-at-home sort of Sunday if you can and take the opportunity to address any outstanding family concerns? Preparing yourself for events that lie ahead is also useful, since forward planning can make things less of an ordeal.

28 MONDAY *Moon Age Day 16 Moon Sign Leo*

The lunar low continues into the start of the new working week. The time of the month when the Moon occupies your opposite zodiac sign isn't ideal for making progress. Be ready to put more effort into decision making and your interactions with other people. It's a question of not allowing yourself to be derailed.

29 TUESDAY *Moon Age Day 17 Moon Sign Virgo*

Confidence is all you need to keep pushing on. Although the lunar low has moved on, direct progress might still be difficult, though forward planning should be possible. Determination is the key, though it's also important to take some time out to simply enjoy yourself, in the company of those close to you.

30 WEDNESDAY *Moon Age Day 18 Moon Sign Virgo*

It's up to you to respond appropriately in any dealings you have with relatives and friends. Make full use of your razor-sharp intuition and ensure you are equal to just about anyone's tricks. Your strong sense of humour can also be a valuable resource under current planetary influences.

31 THURSDAY *Moon Age Day 19 Moon Sign Virgo*

Being asked for advice by those around you can be flattering, though it can sometimes lead to some awkwardness. It's possible that your loyalties could be tested, leaving you in a somewhat difficult position. The general trends in a material sense are favourable.

February
2013

1 FRIDAY *Moon Age Day 20 Moon Sign Libra*

There is much to be said for getting to grips with certain facts and figures at present, though that might not leave too much time for relaxation today. Trends encourage you to focus on practical matters, making this an ideal time for planning some significant changes in and around your home.

2 SATURDAY *Moon Age Day 21 Moon Sign Libra*

Life can have its emotional downside, which is why your interests are best served by getting any personal disputes out of the way as soon as possible. This is not a day during which you should dwell on things or take matters out of context. Ask yourself whether your level of sensitivity might be a little too high right now.

3 SUNDAY *Moon Age Day 22 Moon Sign Scorpio*

You can afford to become more competitive in your dealings with the world in general. Your current creativity should assist you to take on projects that demonstrate your personal flair, even if you don't think you have one. Any confusion over details at work can be easily resolved if you talk things through.

4 MONDAY *Moon Age Day 23 Moon Sign Scorpio*

Relationship issues could well try your patience today and might even seem as though they are more trouble than they are worth. Rather than avoiding serious issues, don't be afraid to be both determined and bold when it counts the most. It's important that you let others know exactly how you feel.

5 TUESDAY *Moon Age Day 24 Moon Sign Sagittarius*

When it comes to making an impact on others, you should already be making this month your own. There are a few astrological reasons why this is encouraged, not least the Sun's present position in your solar first house. Showing people generally what makes you tick could be the easiest task of all.

6 WEDNESDAY *Moon Age Day 25 Moon Sign Sagittarius*

Keep sight of practical necessities and don't allow yourself to be browbeaten into situations that are not of your own personal choosing. Today works best if you can find some space to think things through, though that might not be easy. It's important to gain a true picture of your successes – which may be better than you think!

7 THURSDAY *Moon Age Day 26 Moon Sign Capricorn*

Working towards moderate expectations would be sensible today, and it's worth keeping some of your ideas to yourself. Although it's good to share, there's a danger of losing your edge if you give too much away to others. Casual conversation is fine, as is finding ways to please family members.

8 FRIDAY *Moon Age Day 27 Moon Sign Capricorn*

Even if confidence isn't at its highest, your strong sense of purpose should assist you in any new ventures you begin at this time. It pays to seek support, particularly from colleagues and friends. The Moon in your solar twelfth house may not be too much help, but you have the ability to manage somehow.

9 SATURDAY *Moon Age Day 28 Moon Sign Aquarius*

The lunar high is a time to show the enticing and exciting side of your character, and to use this to attract converts to just about any cause you decide to follow. You can also capitalise on the general good luck that is available and can afford to speculate at least a little. An ideal time for journeys of any sort.

10 SUNDAY *Moon Age Day 0 Moon Sign Aquarius*

With today comes the desire to make a real push towards change, both practically and personally. Fresh starts are very important now and allow you scope to spread your wings, particularly in terms of journeys. If minor setbacks do arise, bear in mind that they could have a positive side.

11 MONDAY *Moon Age Day 1 Moon Sign Pisces*

It's all too easy to allow pressing emotional issues to get in the way of practical progress at the beginning of this new working week. Your best approach is to avoid getting too worked up about anything. You need to realise that any apparent woes will probably turn out to be quite insignificant in the longer term.

12 TUESDAY *Moon Age Day 2 Moon Sign Pisces*

Be prepared to consider making sacrifices in intimate relationships. This shouldn't be too difficult for you, though it might mean having to eat a certain amount of humble pie regarding the way you have dealt with things in the past. Make the most of good news that is available now, probably before the weekend.

13 WEDNESDAY *Moon Age Day 3 Moon Sign Pisces*

Making compromises is the order of the day right now and can help you to forge better relationships all round. You have what it takes to make this a reasonably comfortable sort of day, whether or not it turns out to be a particularly successful one. Can a specific problem be shelved, or even passed on to someone else?

14 THURSDAY *Moon Age Day 4 Moon Sign Aries*

The accent is very much on your personality today, assisting you to give a good account of yourself in all social situations. You can't expect everyone to be on your side at present, but you can at least seek support from the people who matter the most. Even if today isn't extraordinary, it can be quite useful to you.

15 FRIDAY *Moon Age Day 5 Moon Sign Aries*

Being in the limelight could certainly appeal to you a great deal now. That isn't too surprising because Aquarius is an Air sign, and Air signs are typified by a degree of popularity. Getting your own way in social situations should be both easy and fun. Trends assist you to succeed in whatever you turn your hand to now.

16 SATURDAY *Moon Age Day 6 Moon Sign Taurus*

There's nothing wrong with seeking help and support today, even from people you don't know very well. It's a question of using your intuition, which is well marked at present, and which should help you to decide whether someone is worthy of your trust. It can also be useful if you decide to do some shopping.

17 SUNDAY *Moon Age Day 7 Moon Sign Taurus*

Routines have their place, although that doesn't mean you always enjoy them. Your desire for change and diversity is emphasised now, though this might not be too easy to fulfil. However, even little alterations to your daily routines can help. Arranging a social event could also prove a positive distraction.

18 MONDAY *Moon Age Day 8 Moon Sign Gemini*

There is much to be said for doing things for yourself, particularly if you don't feel happy about relying on others now. You may decide to reorder your schedules to leave time for possibilities that are only now coming into your mind. Be ready and willing to react to what is going on around you.

19 TUESDAY *Moon Age Day 9 Moon Sign Gemini*

Appointments may have to be altered at short notice, and you also need to be prepared to deal with any interruptions that come along today. You needn't allow such minor inconveniences to spoil what should be an otherwise steady and happy sort of day. Your competitive side is gradually coming to the fore.

20 WEDNESDAY *Moon Age Day 10 Moon Sign Gemini*

There are good reasons today to seek out people who can be helpful to you, especially individuals who are experts in their own particular field. Once you have found them, you need to gain their support. Socially speaking, trends assist you to be on great form, and to move heaven and earth to have fun.

21 THURSDAY *Moon Age Day 11 Moon Sign Cancer*

Whatever you are doing today, it's important to be sure of your facts before you get going. Current planetary influences indicate a tendency to hesitate somewhat. Rather than giving the impression that you have doubts, your best approach is to put on a confident face and push ahead all the same.

22 FRIDAY *Moon Age Day 12 Moon Sign Cancer*

Much of what happens at the moment is down to your own imagination. With a fairly neutral day on offer, yet plenty of ability to have a bearing on circumstances, this is a chance to show the inventive side of your character. Even if today isn't exactly exciting, you can at least make sure it is eventful.

23 SATURDAY ☿ *Moon Age Day 13 Moon Sign Leo*

You have potential to be very reactive today, and there are signs that if you spend too much time doing only what is expected of you, boredom is possible. Despite the lunar low, variety is the spice of your life now, and it's up to you find it. Aquarius is on the move, even if you don't know where you are going yet.

24 SUNDAY ☿ *Moon Age Day 14 Moon Sign Leo*

Once you have made up your mind about an issue, you needn't allow anyone to alter your opinions. Perhaps just a little more flexibility would be no bad thing, together with a willingness to discuss matters at greater length. As the lunar low continues, planning rather than action is the order of the day.

25 MONDAY ☿ *Moon Age Day 15 Moon Sign Leo*

You would be wise to pay attention to what is happening around you in the world at large. Aquarius can benefit from keeping its ears and eyes wide open now and by using its ability to react to circumstances quickly. Family rows are best avoided, even if this means doing things beyond your own abode.

26 TUESDAY ☿ *Moon Age Day 16 Moon Sign Virgo*

Those Aquarians who have been looking for love now find themselves in a potentially favourable position. This would be an ideal time to persuade the object of your affection to fall in line with your wishes. In a more practical sense, there are gains to be made from looking carefully at work situations and conditions.

27 WEDNESDAY ☿ *Moon Age Day 17 Moon Sign Virgo*

If you find that standard responses to others don't work very well today, you should be willing to adapt to suit prevailing circumstances. Fortunately, that isn't usually difficult for Aquarius. It pays to keep an eye on younger family members, especially if you think they are experiencing some small problems.

28 THURSDAY ☿ *Moon Age Day 18 Moon Sign Libra*

Whatever the weather is doing now, getting out into the fresh air can work wonders. Staying cooped up all the time is no good for Aquarius, and you can gain a new perspective standing on a windy hill or a deserted seashore. This week brings positive challenges, but for now you can afford to relax.

March

2013

1 FRIDAY ☿ *Moon Age Day 19 Moon Sign Libra*

It's natural to feel that certain routines aren't particularly worthy or interesting, but you need to understand that they still have to be addressed. Bear in mind that everyone has problems from time to time, and this can affect how they react to other people. Avoid taking an over-suspicious attitude at this time.

2 SATURDAY ☿ *Moon Age Day 20 Moon Sign Scorpio*

It's possible that settling for the most convenient path won't be enough for you today. You will no doubt find all sorts of jobs if you are determined to dash around from pillar to post. However, is this really necessary? It's your time to waste, though you could put it to better use if you analyse what needs doing, and make a list.

3 SUNDAY ☿ *Moon Age Day 21 Moon Sign Scorpio*

A quieter day is on offer today. Even if life itself isn't any less eventful, it's a question of how you are dealing with the situation. The Moon is in your solar twelfth house, encouraging a more thoughtful and perhaps slightly dreamy interlude. This probably isn't the best day for getting things done.

4 MONDAY ☿ *Moon Age Day 22 Moon Sign Sagittarius*

The start of the new working week is a time to push forward. Make the most of your available energy, as well as your sense of humour. Being in the right place to have a significant bearing on situations can make all the difference, and you can afford to back your hunches. Romance is well starred by the evening.

5 TUESDAY ☿ *Moon Age Day 23 Moon Sign Sagittarius*

Hoping for the best is all very well, though it might not be quite good enough. A little extra effort would certainly help, especially in social situations. This is an ideal time for planning ahead, and for allaying any doubts you sense in others. Be prepared to respond if certain people prove unreliable.

6 WEDNESDAY ☿ *Moon Age Day 24 Moon Sign Sagittarius*

Today works best if you keep up a rather hectic pace and show that you are willing to put in some extra effort to capitalise on all that is happening around you. A certain restless streak is indicated, and you decide it would be distinctly advantageous to do something different, especially towards the close of the day.

7 THURSDAY ☿ *Moon Age Day 25 Moon Sign Capricorn*

Why not make this a special day for yourself and your nearest and dearest? This is an ideal time to plan a treat or simply spend more time with loved ones. The rewards could be great and you can glean satisfaction from knowing that you've helped others through their day. Meetings with friends are favoured later.

8 FRIDAY ☿ *Moon Age Day 26 Moon Sign Capricorn*

A period of relative stability can be achieved today, which might be welcome if the past few days have offered plenty of twists and turns. Even if you find plenty to keep you occupied at this time, there is much to be said for taking a break. Doing so should give you the chance to review recent events and plan new ones.

9 SATURDAY ☿ *Moon Age Day 27 Moon Sign Aquarius*

Making headway is the order of the day now as the lunar high arrives. You might find it difficult to create as many positive opportunities as you wish in a financial sense, but when it comes to having a good time, it's up to you to show that you have fun coming out of your ears! Make sure vitality is your middle name.

10 SUNDAY ☿ *Moon Age Day 28 Moon Sign Aquarius*

The favourable trends continue, assisting you in your efforts to get the response you want from others. This is unlikely to be a stay-at-home sort of Sunday. On the contrary, your interests are best served if you make as many changes as possible, even if that means making some sort of impromptu journey.

11 MONDAY ☿ *Moon Age Day 29 Moon Sign Pisces*

It pays to put your fun-loving side on show today. The start of this new working week offers scope for plenty of joking, particularly if you allow your natural sense of humour to work overtime. Any aches and pains you experience right now are probably in your sides – from laughing so much!

12 TUESDAY ☿ *Moon Age Day 0 Moon Sign Pisces*

Success today is about feeling useful and completing any tasks that have been outstanding in your life for some time. If you manage to do this, you should be able to free up more time to please yourself, maybe to commence some sort of project you have been dreaming about for many months.

13 WEDNESDAY ☿ *Moon Age Day 1 Moon Sign Aries*

You can't expect every item on your agenda to work out quite the way you had been expecting. Be prepared to review the situation and start again. Your level of patience is highlighted at the moment, and it shouldn't really matter how many times you have to recommence. All that matters is moving forward.

14 THURSDAY ☿ *Moon Age Day 2 Moon Sign Aries*

Along comes a time of genuine romantic potential. To make the most of this you really need to find exactly the right words to say 'I love you', even to people who might not generally be very receptive. Your natural curiosity is in play now, assisting you to investigate almost anything that takes your fancy.

15 FRIDAY ☿ *Moon Age Day 3 Moon Sign Taurus*

A day to get as much variety into your life as you can manage. Allowing yourself to become stuck in any sort of rut is not to be recommended. The fact is that Aquarius needs a great deal of stimulation, and you have what it takes to obtain this through intellectual knockabouts with the world at large.

16 SATURDAY ☿ *Moon Age Day 4 Moon Sign Taurus*

If unexpected obligations come along, there isn't much you can do except respond to them in the best way you can. Everyone feels tired from time to time, and today there is no shame in deciding to take a break. Once you feel better, you should be able to function far more efficiently as a result.

17 SUNDAY ☿ *Moon Age Day 5 Moon Sign Taurus*

This is an ideal time to focus on specific details you know you will have to attend to sooner or later. It would be far better to get them behind you as soon as possible, leaving more time for enjoyment later in the day. Be ready to show just how much work you can actually get through at this time, and with maximum efficiency.

18 MONDAY ☿ *Moon Age Day 6 Moon Sign Gemini*

You have an opportunity to discover that attracting the good things in life is a piece of cake this Monday, but even cake can be sickening after a while. There's nothing wrong with deliberately seeking a little solitude. You might extend that to being with people you know and love, though possibly not strangers today.

19 TUESDAY *Moon Age Day 7 Moon Sign Gemini*

A potentially hectic phase is available, and one that requires all the attention you can muster. One possible consequence is fatigue. Even if you don't suffer too much with tiredness as a rule, you do have your limits. An early night, or a relaxing couple of hours chatting with friends, can work wonders.

20 WEDNESDAY *Moon Age Day 8 Moon Sign Cancer*

You have scope for some advancement today, though if it is of the slow and steady sort it might not be quick enough to please you. Varying your routines as much as possible can make all the difference, and helps you to avoid the sort of boredom that can sometimes come upon you.

21 THURSDAY *Moon Age Day 9 Moon Sign Cancer*

Trends suggest this is unlikely to be the most dynamic day ever, and it would be sensible to lower yourself into the water slowly, especially where new incentives at work are concerned. By all means look for ways to increase your financial wherewithal, though be aware that you shouldn't expect immediate results.

22 FRIDAY *Moon Age Day 10 Moon Sign Cancer*

Now you can capitalise on an influx of bright and interesting new ideas. The Sun enters your solar third house, encouraging constructive thinking and positive action. Especially as this is a Friday, it's worth looking for ways to make life sing. Making improvements in a professional sense could be more difficult.

23 SATURDAY *Moon Age Day 11 Moon Sign Leo*

This is a day when keeping a low profile is your best approach. The Moon is in your opposite sign and doing you no real favours. You can afford to spend some relaxation time with friends or family members. However, you need to make certain that you are not being expected to run any show single-handedly.

24 SUNDAY *Moon Age Day 12 Moon Sign Leo*

Despite the lunar low, today offers some light-hearted moments and the chance to display your sense of humour to the world. Confidence shouldn't be lacking, though your ability to get where you want to be could be somewhat restricted. You need to find a balance between your social life and time spent with your family.

25 MONDAY *Moon Age Day 13 Moon Sign Virgo*

Bear in mind that if other people don't fulfil their obligations, the result could well reflect on you. It's up to you to tackle such situations, though you can't expect to please everyone if you decide to do so. Remember that you're not speaking out just for the sake of it. Is there really any reason to feel bad about your actions?

26 TUESDAY *Moon Age Day 14 Moon Sign Virgo*

Trends assist you to manage a dozen different jobs at the same time today and still come out on top. Don't simply assume that help will pour from every direction. By all means try to persuade people to be part of your dreams and schemes, though be prepared to admit that there isn't much point in arguing.

27 WEDNESDAY *Moon Age Day 15 Moon Sign Libra*

If mundane and domestic matters prove tiresome today, ask yourself whether you really need to involve yourself with them at all if you can help it. This is an ideal time for Aquarians who haven't felt at their best across the last week or so to look for signs of improvement and make the most of the energy that is available.

28 THURSDAY *Moon Age Day 16 Moon Sign Libra*

Make the most of today's potential by finding people who can stimulate your mind simply by talking to you. The focus is also on romance, though as is so often the case for Aquarius, this could well turn out to be affection of the temporary sort rather than that which is necessary for a strong lifetime commitment.

29 FRIDAY *Moon Age Day 17 Moon Sign Libra*

Any association with communications is well accented at present. Whether you are the one doing the talking, or it's you that is listening to others, it is only through co-operation that anything much is achieved. There is no reason for your working life to be tedious at present, and you can afford to show a happy face to the world at large.

30 SATURDAY *Moon Age Day 18 Moon Sign Scorpio*

Keeping ahead of the crowd seems to be the name of the game for you right now, so you may decide that the weekend isn't the time for rest and relaxation. If you can't move forward with current projects, there's nothing wrong with inventing a whole new raft of ideas, intentions and adventures.

31 SUNDAY *Moon Age Day 19 Moon Sign Scorpio*

You have a chance to make this Sunday your own by turning directly away from routines and looking for something exciting to do. Rather than tiring yourself early in the day, it's worth spreading your energy evenly throughout the morning and afternoon. Be ready to trip the light fantastic in the evening.

April

2013

1 MONDAY *Moon Age Day 20 Moon Sign Sagittarius*

'Get cracking' is the planetary message now. This would be a good day to capitalise on recent fresh starts. Prepare to be asked to make up your mind quickly regarding current projects, which may mean rapid forward motion, combined with maximum analysis. Under these trends you have what it takes to achieve this combination.

2 TUESDAY *Moon Age Day 21 Moon Sign Sagittarius*

Progress today is a question of quickening the pace of life and realising just how much you have to offer. Don't be too quick to jump to conclusions, especially where affairs of the heart are concerned. You need to look at different possibilities today, using a mixture of common sense and intuition.

3 WEDNESDAY *Moon Age Day 22 Moon Sign Capricorn*

You can attract positive reactions from the individuals you encounter today and might also be able to discover a few well-kept secrets. The chatty and curious side of the Aquarius nature is emphasised, assisting you to achieve a rapport with many different types of people. By all means push yourself – though not too far!

4 THURSDAY *Moon Age Day 23 Moon Sign Capricorn*

There may be quite an ego boost available in a social sense. There are signs that you could be very much in demand at the moment, and this state of affairs could well become more obvious as the day wears on. Communication skills are well accented, and there is humour to be found in most situations.

5 FRIDAY *Moon Age Day 24 Moon Sign Aquarius*

It's time to back your hunches because the lunar high gives you everything you need to get Lady Luck on your side now. Be prepared to stick with your decisions today and show a more decisive face to the world than has been the case for a few days past. Make sure you leave some free time for simply having fun.

6 SATURDAY *Moon Age Day 25 Moon Sign Aquarius*

It's full steam ahead as all the positive influences in your chart come together to help you create a cracking day. Of course you cannot expect everyone to be on your side, but you can persuade those people who really count to help you. Confidence is enhanced, and this can assist you to improve your earning potential.

7 SUNDAY *Moon Age Day 26 Moon Sign Pisces*

Your ideal response to today would be to keep on the move. You needn't allow yourself to be held back by anything at this time, not even particularly demanding relatives. Routines can be a bore, especially if they involve you spending long periods of time in the same place. Why not simply avoid them for now?

8 MONDAY *Moon Age Day 27 Moon Sign Pisces*

Where you have most potential to win out today is in attracting the material things of life. You probably won't want to spend all your time working, and can afford to take some time out to enjoy yourself. If your finances are in a better state than expected, there's nothing wrong with spending a little. A treat can work wonders.

9 TUESDAY *Moon Age Day 28 Moon Sign Aries*

You would be wise to think very carefully about personal decisions. There is much to be said for seeking advice from someone in the know, and actually taking it on board. If you want to change aspects of your personal life, you need to consult your partner, rather than going ahead without thinking.

10 WEDNESDAY *Moon Age Day 0 Moon Sign Aries*

Along comes a socially uplifting trend and a time when you have everything you need to attract just the right sort of people into your life. Group-based activities are especially well highlighted at this time, assisting you to stand up and speak in public. Under current trends, you might actually welcome the opportunity!

11 THURSDAY *Moon Age Day 1 Moon Sign Aries*

If specific emotional issues are uppermost in your mind, it could be somewhat awkward to concentrate on those things that you know you should be doing in a practical sense. Today is a chance to put your anxieties on the back burner. By the time you get round to looking at them again, they might even have disappeared.

12 FRIDAY *Moon Age Day 2 Moon Sign Taurus*

Talks and general encounters with others ought to be part of what this Friday is about. Be willing to think ahead and maybe stay still for a few hours, even if a restless streak is still upon you. The more you mull things over today, the better you are going to get on in the longer term.

13 SATURDAY *Moon Age Day 3 Moon Sign Taurus*

This has potential to be a favourable weekend from a domestic perspective, with few restrictions to hold you back. Getting out and about would be no bad thing, particularly if you can do so in the company of family members. Give yourself credit for a success that is becoming more obvious with each passing day.

14 SUNDAY *Moon Age Day 4 Moon Sign Gemini*

You may need to focus your ideas better, especially when it is necessary for you to share them with others. Explaining yourself is the key today, and this Sunday represents an interlude when you have everything you need to get what you want. Simply turn on that famous Aquarian charm.

15 MONDAY *Moon Age Day 5 Moon Sign Gemini*

There are pleasant encounters on offer today, not least with people you haven't seen for some time. Catching up with the past is part of your present, and seems to be quite important to you now. Dull and boring routines are probably best avoided now because they have little to offer you at this time.

16 TUESDAY *Moon Age Day 6 Moon Sign Gemini*

Trends suggest there is something of the pioneer about you today. Remember that the desire to get new things up and running requires patience and balance, qualities that could be in rather short supply just for the moment. It might be better to restrict yourself to less demanding jobs and continue the search for fun.

17 WEDNESDAY *Moon Age Day 7 Moon Sign Cancer*

You need to focus on the quality of experiences at the moment and certainly not the quantity. If you've been burning the candle at both ends for a while, don't be surprised if you suddenly find yourself collapsing in a heap. Social influences are still favourable, though a relaxed sort of encounter works best.

18 THURSDAY *Moon Age Day 8 Moon Sign Cancer*

Places of entertainment have a great deal to offer today. You need diversion and can find it in a host of different places. Tying yourself to a particular place or routine, to the exclusion of all else, is not to be recommended at the moment. The most important thing today is to keep talking.

19 FRIDAY *Moon Age Day 9 Moon Sign Leo*

The lunar low does little to boost your energy, and makes it difficult for you to use the inventive and quick quality that sets your zodiac sign apart. Use this period to recharge your batteries and don't expect to move any mountains. If you insist on pushing against planetary trends, exhaustion could well be the result.

20 SATURDAY *Moon Age Day 10 Moon Sign Leo*

Be prepared to reap the benefits of applying a lighter touch when it comes to discussions and encounters with others. Even if you have slowed the general pace of life somewhat during the lunar low, such is the array of positive planets in your chart at the moment that you might be able to ignore its presence.

21 SUNDAY *Moon Age Day 11 Moon Sign Leo*

Once again, energy and general spirits might be low, and it's worth finding some way today to cheer yourself up. Negative types are best avoided, as are people who constantly make demands of you but offer nothing at all in return. You do have confidence – but it may be rather buried for the moment.

22 MONDAY *Moon Age Day 12 Moon Sign Virgo*

Trends assist you to keep a high profile, especially in social settings. The focus is on your natural urge to take a hands-on approach to almost any situation, and you probably won't be happy to let others live your life for you. Think seriously about any binding commitments you're entering around this period.

23 TUESDAY *Moon Age Day 13 Moon Sign Virgo*

Harmonious situations are all very well, though there's a chance you might actually find life to be somewhat dull now. If this turns out to be the case, you need to look to your own actions. In material matters and where decisions have to be made, take the bull by the horns. Your decision making is well accented now.

24 WEDNESDAY *Moon Age Day 14 Moon Sign Libra*

Be prepared to deal with setbacks when it comes to making decisions today. You can't expect everyone to share the same point of view and to offer identical advice, and therein lies the problem. It's a question of deciding for yourself, even if one or two people directly disagree with your final conclusions.

25 THURSDAY *Moon Age Day 15 Moon Sign Libra*

Assistance can be obtained from some unexpected places, especially when it comes to any issue involving money. Meanwhile, you have what it takes to show a very social face to the world and to get on well with others, even those who haven't been your cup of tea in the past. Plan now for an excursion at the weekend.

26 FRIDAY *Moon Age Day 16 Moon Sign Scorpio*

Positive thinking can help you enormously at present in terms of progress. Even if you encounter the odd setback today, you should still be moving forward in a general sense. A growing desire to throw off the fetters of conventional thinking becomes apparent, though this is nothing too unusual for Aquarius.

27 SATURDAY *Moon Age Day 17 Moon Sign Scorpio*

You have scope to make some interesting things happen today, particularly with regard to your love life. In addition, the very real effort that others put in your behalf should help you to feel generally good about yourself. Any confidences you gather at present must be carefully guarded.

28 SUNDAY *Moon Age Day 18 Moon Sign Sagittarius*

It's worth remembering that it is impossible to please all of the people, all of the time. Despite this realisation, you might be tempted to try to do so at some stage today. Conciliation and arbitration are hallmarks of your zodiac sign. Be prepared to deal with any particularly awkward people you encounter at the moment.

29 MONDAY *Moon Age Day 19 Moon Sign Sagittarius*

Work and practical progress should be easy enough to deal with. Avoid allowing others to pressure you. Even if this isn't a problem now, you should keep it in mind for the whole of the week. Start as you mean to go on and let people know just how far you are willing to bend in any given situation.

30 TUESDAY *Moon Age Day 20 Moon Sign Capricorn*

Today offers you a chance to give emotional assistance to any loved ones who need it. Aquarius's willingness to listen is to the fore, supporting the efforts you make for the sake of those around you. Even if conforming to expectations in a work sense isn't very easy, would it hurt you to try?

May

2013

1 WEDNESDAY *Moon Age Day 21 Moon Sign Capricorn*

Be ready to respond if that old friend of Aquarius, restlessness, pays you a visit now. Your best approach is to keep busy and to think up new schemes that you find both stimulating and potentially rewarding. If you're looking for entertaining people, pals you've known for a long time would be a good place to start.

2 THURSDAY *Moon Age Day 22 Moon Sign Aquarius*

This is one of the best days of the month for getting your own way, and you shouldn't have to bully anyone. The lunar high assists you to show how charming and approachable you can be, while at the same time enhancing the natural dominance that allows you to persuade others to fall in line with your wishes.

3 FRIDAY *Moon Age Day 23 Moon Sign Aquarius*

There's no doubt about it: self-belief is the name of the game today and the position of the Moon in your own zodiac sign is a great help. Keep faith with each of the decisions and moves you make. Showing a high level of confidence will assist you to obtain more help than you could possibly need.

4 SATURDAY *Moon Age Day 24 Moon Sign Pisces*

If you have a single fault at present, it might be that you are scattering your energies too much. A little more concentration can make all the difference just now, together with some specific follow-through in certain situations. All of this could be somewhat wasted advice if you are simply determined to do anything that pleases you today.

5 SUNDAY *Moon Age Day 25 Moon Sign Pisces*

Though the general trends surrounding home and family seem to be as favourable now as they have been for quite a while, that doesn't mean you won't be rather restless on occasion today. Try to do something different and spend time with friends. Who knows? This could spark some interesting ideas.

6 MONDAY *Moon Age Day 26 Moon Sign Pisces*

Your persuasive tongue can be extremely useful now. There are gains to be made by convincing others to do your bidding, and you can ensure they will benefit too. Part of this process is explaining your reasoning. If you approach situations correctly, opposition from other people shouldn't be an issue.

7 TUESDAY *Moon Age Day 27 Moon Sign Aries*

Where plans and schemes generally are concerned this is clearly a time to be taking an independent route. If you don't think others have the answers you need, now is the time to tell them so. There may well be certain responsibilities today that you can't shirk, and it's worth getting them out of the way early in the day.

8 WEDNESDAY *Moon Age Day 28 Moon Sign Aries*

A day to enjoy some good company. Once again, getting all necessary tasks out of the way as soon as possible would be no bad thing. This is the Air-sign way, and it helps you to assess how much time remains to do the things you wish. You would be wise to monitor the behaviour of younger family members.

9 THURSDAY *Moon Age Day 29 Moon Sign Taurus*

Even if you manage to get specific professional matters to bear fruit now, it might be more difficult for you to make progress in personal issues. Part of the problem is that it's not always easy to say the right thing. However, you need to ask yourself whether you are the one who is causing the problem.

10 FRIDAY *Moon Age Day 0 Moon Sign Taurus*

A great sense of security is available to you today. This could prove quite important, particularly if you feel you are falling short of your own expectations at present. Seeking not only encouragement, but also love, from your nearest and dearest can make all the difference. Try not to push yourself too hard.

11 SATURDAY *Moon Age Day 1 Moon Sign Gemini*

By all means keep yourself very active today, though bear in mind that getting exactly what you want from life may not be too easy. The first step will be to persuade others that you have a valid point of view and that you know what you are doing. It pays to seek support from friends rather than colleagues.

12 SUNDAY *Moon Age Day 2 Moon Sign Gemini*

Be ready for comings and goings aplenty today, encouraging you to keep on the move from morning until night. Although you might find it difficult to bring certain people round to your particular point of view, in the main you should have little difficulty getting your particular message across.

13 MONDAY *Moon Age Day 3 Moon Sign Gemini*

The spotlight is now on personal matters, though you needn't allow these to detract from your efforts to gain ground in more practical arenas. When it comes to sport, you have what it takes to put on an excellent show at the moment. If you aren't involved in any such activities, now is an ideal time to think about them.

14 TUESDAY *Moon Age Day 4 Moon Sign Cancer*

You can make the most of the high spirits and energy that are available today by striking while the iron's hot. Important activities are indicated, though you might need to persuade others to get involved. Before you commit yourself, you would be wise to make sure that you are not going to offer any unintentional offence.

15 WEDNESDAY *Moon Age Day 5 Moon Sign Cancer*

Domestic matters take on a new importance under current influences, and at the same time there are signs that at least a part of your mind is dwelling in the past. Focusing on all sorts of minor issues is all very well, though there's a risk you might overcrowd your intellect somewhat. Try to calm things down.

16 THURSDAY *Moon Age Day 6 Moon Sign Leo*

Be prepared to deal with a few obstacles today. Even if the lunar low isn't very powerful, it will do little to help you to get things going the way you might wish. A conventional approach is the order of the day at present, making it less likely that you will be chasing rainbows in any sphere of your life.

17 FRIDAY *Moon Age Day 7 Moon Sign Leo*

Energy levels may be more limited while the lunar low is around, and if you find this to be the case, it's not worth kicking against it. Today works best if you can keep yourself busy in quiet ways and enjoy the chance to take a break. What a great time this would be to take a walk and watch the flowers grow!

18 SATURDAY *Moon Age Day 8 Moon Sign Leo*

In terms of communication you can capitalise on plenty of potential today. Little Mercury is positively placed in your chart, aiding your ability to say what you really think, though without offering offence to anyone in your vicinity. It's time to show the people you meet just how charming you can be.

19 SUNDAY *Moon Age Day 9 Moon Sign Virgo*

For those of you who are looking for advancement, or even a new career path, life could seem rather sluggish. Planetary trends now are geared more specifically towards your personal life and the less material elements of life. However, there is nothing to prevent you from thinking hard now, ahead of action later.

20 MONDAY *Moon Age Day 10 Moon Sign Virgo*

Challenges in general life situations are now a distinct possibility. Perhaps you need to deal with demands from loved ones, or maybe you simply can't find your way forward through reams of red tape. It would be best to relax and to wait and see whether you can change your attitude and approach to matters as the day passes.

21 TUESDAY *Moon Age Day 11 Moon Sign Libra*

An ideal day to seek the information you really need, from either your partner or your friends. Eliciting help from colleagues could prove especially difficult, and you need to ask yourself whether your own recent actions have anything to do with the attitude of others. Avoid being quick to anger in any confrontation.

22 WEDNESDAY *Moon Age Day 12 Moon Sign Libra*

You have what it takes to attract a friendly response from most people right now, and this can help you to achieve some positive objectives. Having fun is the name of the game, and there is much to be said for leaving material concerns on the shelf for the moment. Allow friends to boost your personal confidence.

23 THURSDAY *Moon Age Day 13 Moon Sign Scorpio*

Potential ego-boosting power is on offer now that the Sun is entering your solar fifth house. Love and romance are especially susceptible to this trend, and sons and daughters of Aquarius can turn this day into something really special. That doesn't mean you should forget your working life. It's time to pep it up if you can!

24 FRIDAY *Moon Age Day 14 Moon Sign Scorpio*

Trends assist you to increase your sense of security and belonging by focusing on emotional and domestic matters. If Aquarians feel snug and warm inside their lives, outside matters tend to take care of themselves. Bear in mind that seeking some timely assistance is not a sign of failure.

25 SATURDAY *Moon Age Day 15 Moon Sign Sagittarius*

Family members have it in them to make you feel a great deal more comfortable. Whether or not you can persuade them to exercise this ability remains to be seen and is tied, in part, to your own attitude. Be prepared to offer incentives that imply trust, particularly in the case of younger relatives.

26 SUNDAY *Moon Age Day 16 Moon Sign Sagittarius*

You can afford to put a few responsibilities to one side today while you decide to have some fun. It's natural to feel somewhat concerned at the behaviour of those closest to you. There is much to be said for using the current interlude to take those concerned out of themselves, and that can be a remedy for almost any ill.

27 MONDAY *Moon Age Day 17 Moon Sign Capricorn*

Trends highlight your natural curiosity and your desire to broaden your horizons. This offers an opportunity to enjoy another day that responds well to changes of scenery. Give and take proves to be important in personal matters, but you can still get your own way, and without upsetting any apple carts.

28 TUESDAY *Moon Age Day 18 Moon Sign Capricorn*

Pressures in your social life are a distinct possibility, particularly if having to do the same old thing is causing boredom. It's time to ring the changes, even though to do so might not please everyone. There is much to be said for allowing the individualist within you to show its face as soon as possible.

29 WEDNESDAY *Moon Age Day 19 Moon Sign Aquarius*

The lunar high is an ideal time to try to get your own way with others. You shouldn't have to work very hard to get where you want to be today, especially if you tap into the support that's on offer. Try to get as much variety into your life as possible, and be willing to make yourself the centre of attention in your immediate circle.

30 THURSDAY *Moon Age Day 20 Moon Sign Aquarius*

This is the best time of the month for making new starts and for taking chances of almost any sort. Make sure you show people your potential, and use this to create new contacts and a high degree of popularity. Use the power of today's lunar high to dispel any recent fog of confusion that you've experienced.

31 FRIDAY *Moon Age Day 21 Moon Sign Aquarius*

Making room for personal indulgences would be no bad thing today. Aquarius doesn't usually go in for a life of luxury, but it is good to spoil yourself once in a while. Although the lunar high is starting to fade, you should still be showing that irrepressible energy that is a natural aspect of your life now.

June 2013

1 SATURDAY *Moon Age Day 22 Moon Sign Pisces*

This is a particularly favourable day to get out into the social mainstream, and to enjoy the fruits of past labours. Some attention to finance is necessary if you want to ensure you aren't spending more than is coming in. This may not matter in the short term, but you will need to get your practical head on before long.

2 SUNDAY *Moon Age Day 23 Moon Sign Pisces*

Trends suggest that choosing peace and quiet at home might not be the best use of what today offers. It's time to capitalise on your current popularity, and to take advantage of the attention and invitations you have available to you. Bear in mind that you can't do everything, and there's nothing wrong with a polite refusal if necessary.

3 MONDAY *Moon Age Day 24 Moon Sign Aries*

Even if you are keeping up a hurried pace, particularly at work, you should still find the time to socialise and to look at romance in a bigger way than has been possible for a while. You have what it takes to attract some great compliments at present, though you will have to pay attention if you don't want to miss them!

4 TUESDAY *Moon Age Day 25 Moon Sign Aries*

You have the potential to shine personally today and you needn't allow anything to prevent you from doing so. Any uninteresting jobs are best dealt with early in the day and then you can concentrate on what pleases you. Be ready to deal with aspects of the past that come back to haunt you. Simply smile and carry on.

5 WEDNESDAY *Moon Age Day 26 Moon Sign Taurus*

Self-reliance is very important at this time. All the same, what matters the most right now is not what others can do for you, but rather what you are willing to do for them. The deeper and more spiritual side of your nature is now coming to the fore. Once again the emphasis is on your current popularity, and on how you use it.

6 THURSDAY *Moon Age Day 27 Moon Sign Taurus*

Why not opt for a complete change of scene if you get the chance today? Trends highlight the restless side of your nature, and seeking fresh fields and pastures new can really make the difference. Not that this is at all extraordinary for Aquarius. Simply open your eyes and look at the world – you'll be surprised at what you can find.

7 FRIDAY *Moon Age Day 28 Moon Sign Taurus*

Be prepared to confront some tricky professional matters today. It's easy to think you've got things sorted to your satisfaction, only to find you are back to square one. The present astrological picture highlights such frustrations. Your best approach is to rise above them and be determined to enjoy yourself.

8 SATURDAY *Moon Age Day 0 Moon Sign Gemini*

A little privacy goes a long way, even if you decide to stay in the social limelight now. Cloying people and stifling situations have little to offer you at this stage. You may also feel suffocated by convention, especially if you are a young Aquarian. Sometimes you don't have any real choice except to go with the flow.

9 SUNDAY *Moon Age Day 1 Moon Sign Gemini*

There are gains to be made by putting plenty of energy into getting things done, though you need to be ready to deal with any obstacles in your path. Don't dismiss the opinions of others, since they could provide some useful and important information. Leave boring routines to types who appear to relish them.

10 MONDAY *Moon Age Day 2 Moon Sign Cancer*

Beware of pushing ahead with new ambitions before you have really investigated situations. This is especially relevant where money is concerned. Actually this isn't a particularly favourable time for speculation of any sort, and there are good reasons to put a curb on spending until you have sorted your mind out.

11 TUESDAY *Moon Age Day 3 Moon Sign Cancer*

Professional matters could well go somewhat off course today. Patience is your best response, especially if you're having to repeat yourself a good deal, both in terms of words and deeds. Money matters are reasonably well accented, and you need to plan for better times that are available ahead.

12 WEDNESDAY *Moon Age Day 4 Moon Sign Cancer*

The emphasis at the moment is on fun. Avoid taking yourself or anyone else too seriously at present and be ready to make things go with a swing. If you show how fond you are of fun, you stand a better chance of attracting good company. All of this can assist you to boost your popularity, which can really make a difference.

13 THURSDAY *Moon Age Day 5 Moon Sign Leo*

Whatever you decide to take on board today, remember that energy might be hard to find. Today works best if you choose to stay out of the limelight and spend as many hours as you can doing something quiet. You needn't allow the lunar low to affect personal relationships, which are well starred now.

14 FRIDAY *Moon Age Day 6 Moon Sign Leo*

This isn't the best time of the month for getting ahead in a general sense. Be pleased with minor gains and take time out to reflect. A sentimental and even nostalgic interlude is indicated for Aquarius. The advancing year and summer weather might make this a good time for a walk out of doors.

15 SATURDAY *Moon Age Day 7 Moon Sign Virgo*

There are signs that some emotions are now very close to the surface. A little soul-searching may be in order, particularly in terms of your personal life and the way you are interacting with loved ones at present. However, too much deep thinking is a waste of time, because life is genuinely for living right now.

16 SUNDAY *Moon Age Day 8 Moon Sign Virgo*

Practical issues and run-of-the-mill routines should be easy to deal with this Sunday. Once again the spotlight is on your urge to go to new places and meet people who are fresh to your life. This can be a good time to put original ideas to the test, perhaps by sharing them with people whose company you enjoy.

17 MONDAY *Moon Age Day 9 Moon Sign Virgo*

It's worth listening to the viewpoints and philosophies of those who surround you at this juncture. Even if you know there is much to be done, leaving some of it on the back burner would be no bad thing. Make the most of opportunities for a good gossip, and capitalise on the information you gather.

18 TUESDAY *Moon Age Day 10 Moon Sign Libra*

Exciting social encounters are within your reach today. You may decide to stay away from pointless rules and regulations, particularly if these annoy you. Be prepared to look to friends both for interest and for support as the day wears on. It's time to show the strength of your nature by refusing to retreat from any challenge.

19 WEDNESDAY *Moon Age Day 11 Moon Sign Libra*

A heavily competitive element is indicated now, encouraging you to look at even existing circumstances in a radical way. Losing is unlikely to be on your agenda, whatever the activity, and it pays to keep your mind working overtime on career opportunities. All the same, a little enjoyment can work wonders.

20 THURSDAY *Moon Age Day 12 Moon Sign Scorpio*

You need to ask yourself whether you are missing out somehow in the career stakes, despite the efforts you have made. This would be an ideal time for a reappraisal. If necessary, seek out some professional advice and certainly don't assume that you already know the answer to any problem.

21 FRIDAY *Moon Age Day 13 Moon Sign Scorpio*

Avoid misunderstandings by stating your case from the word go. You'll get the best from today if you manage to make your work less of a chore. This means finding a balance between keeping yourself busy and seeking relaxation later in the day. Have you arranged to do something interesting at the weekend?

22 SATURDAY *Moon Age Day 14 Moon Sign Sagittarius*

Success can be achieved at the moment partly through being well organised. You can fall down if you haven't dealt with eventualities. Don't let opportunities slip by simply because you haven't prepared yourself properly. This would be an ideal time to instigate new business partnerships.

23 SUNDAY *Moon Age Day 15 Moon Sign Sagittarius*

Even if your dealings with others in social settings are somewhat strained, you need to do what you can to make a good impression on friends. Practically speaking, this can be a time of high achievement. Avoid unnecessary discussions about situations that don't interest you and which you cannot alter.

24 MONDAY *Moon Age Day 16 Moon Sign Capricorn*

The spotlight is now on financial stability, and on your willingness to find ways to improve the situation. It's a question of following up on important leads and gathering all the information you can. With a good deal of thought and a little action, you have everything you need to get finances looking much stronger.

25 TUESDAY *Moon Age Day 17 Moon Sign Capricorn*

You have scope to make this a successful time when it comes to love affairs, whether these are of the lifelong variety or simply temporary assignations. In the family sphere, conforming to expectations may not be easy. Tolerance is the order of the day, particularly if you are dealing with younger people.

26 WEDNESDAY *Moon Age Day 18 Moon Sign Aquarius*

Faster, better, more efficient – this is how your mind should be working under the lunar high. There are a bevy of planetary positions and associations helping to spur you on, and there should be nothing to stop you enjoying life to the full. Remember to take some time out to have fun with the people closest to you.

27 THURSDAY ☿ *Moon Age Day 19 Moon Sign Aquarius*

The general trends have plenty to offer you today, especially in any situation that involves you taking the bull by the horns. It's not about leaving things to chance, but about taking advantage of the support available to make your life easier. Good luck is within your grasp, and you might even decide to go for a little flutter.

28 FRIDAY ☿ *Moon Age Day 20 Moon Sign Pisces*

You are encouraged to focus your current energy on breaking through barriers that might have looked high and wide indeed in the recent past. You could even be left wondering why you were intimidated in the first place! It's also time to show how sharp your powers of persuasion and general intellect can be.

29 SATURDAY ☿ *Moon Age Day 21 Moon Sign Pisces*

Aquarius can be the life and soul of the party at the moment. Even if you aren't able to make the forward strides you would wish in a work sense, your natural charm can help you to compensate for this. Bulldozing your way through any obstacle really shouldn't be necessary at this time.

30 SUNDAY ☿ *Moon Age Day 22 Moon Sign Aries*

Be ready to pursue an eventful social life, and to capitalise on constantly improving trends in deeper attachments. Aquarians who are now commencing a new romantic relationship should be able to ensure it now goes from strength to strength. Your strong intuition can be invaluable if decisions have to be made.

July 2013

1 MONDAY ☿ *Moon Age Day 23 Moon Sign Aries*

Try to keep things on an even keel at work and avoid allowing yourself to become distracted by matters you cannot control. Be prepared to seek some timely help and advice, especially from the direction of someone you care about deeply. This is probably not the best day to confront controversial issues if you can help it.

2 TUESDAY ☿ *Moon Age Day 24 Moon Sign Taurus*

There are plenty of opportunities to hog the limelight now, so much so that you might become fed up of smiling! The emphasis is on showing the world what you are made of, and coming up with answers when it matters. If there are any limitations on your nature during present trends, these are probably self-created.

3 WEDNESDAY ☿ *Moon Age Day 25 Moon Sign Taurus*

There are good reasons to find out what other people really feel about you around this time. Obviously it's heartening if the feedback is positive, though your ego can easily be dented if not all responses are exactly what you would wish. You have to come to terms with the fact that not everyone loves you.

4 THURSDAY ☿ *Moon Age Day 26 Moon Sign Taurus*

Make the most of beneficial highlights that are available, particularly at work. Good results can be achieved through practical efforts, and you have what it takes to make the most of all situations today. Love and romance are particularly emphasised now, as is your willingness to gain popularity among your peers.

5 FRIDAY ☿ *Moon Age Day 27 Moon Sign Gemini*

Personal contacts with co-workers might benefit from your attention today, and there is potential for you to make some improvements. There is much to be said for putting behind you any sort of antagonism that has existed previously. This is an ideal time to seek the warmth and companionship of friends.

6 SATURDAY ☿ *Moon Age Day 28 Moon Sign Gemini*

The current planetary focus is on work, and you are encouraged to keep very much on the move today, whether or not you are actually holding down a position at the moment. Socially speaking you have scope to pursue a good time, though it's also worth showing that you have a quieter side to your nature.

7 SUNDAY ☿ *Moon Age Day 0 Moon Sign Cancer*

When it comes to fulfilling the expectations that others have of you, you can be second to none right now, and should be able to convince others of your sincerity in a variety of situations. If you've been burning the candle at both ends, it ought to be possible to get some rest without killing your social life stone dead.

8 MONDAY ☿ *Moon Age Day 1 Moon Sign Cancer*

Trends suggest you might now be up against some strident views, particularly coming from the direction of people you associate with on a day-to-day basis. You would be wise to take life steadily today. There's no reason to become flustered by issues that normally would not bother you in the slightest.

9 TUESDAY ☿ *Moon Age Day 2 Moon Sign Cancer*

Social discussions of almost any sort now have a great deal to offer you. It's natural to be concerned for others, though you also need to recognise the positive progress that certain individuals have made recently. At work you should be aware that there is no shortcut to success. Simply keep ploughing on regardless!

10 WEDNESDAY ☿ *Moon Age Day 3 Moon Sign Leo*

Put any major issues to one side and prepare yourself for an interlude that encourages a quieter approach. This is no bad thing and will allow you some time to think about yourself and projects you are presently planning. Even if you are not currently pursuing a highly charged social life, there could still be offers about.

11 THURSDAY ☿ *Moon Age Day 4 Moon Sign Leo*

The continuing lunar low offers another day that is less than inspiring, so it's important to capitalise on any influence you do have. It's worth seeking support from friends if you need it, in terms of both practical help and interesting information. Slowly but surely, you should be climbing out of your little quiet spell.

12 FRIDAY ☿ *Moon Age Day 5 Moon Sign Virgo*

Positive highlights in relationships can help you to create a generally good day on the personal front. At the same time a distinctly nostalgic mood is indicated, one that encourages your mind far back into the past. Competitive activities can benefit from a strong boost to social matters, together with generally progressive trends.

13 SATURDAY ☿ *Moon Age Day 6 Moon Sign Virgo*

You have what it takes to be a winner at work, and this trend is set to last for a while. This is only really relevant if you are a weekend worker, otherwise you need to put your efforts into your home and social life. Concern for the underdog could be high on the list of Aquarian priorities at this point in time.

14 SUNDAY ☿ *Moon Age Day 7 Moon Sign Virgo*

This is a time when, on the whole, things do go better in pairs. In a general sense it's all very well knowing what you want from life, but you need to recognise that others may have a better idea than you do about how to get it. Remember that a straight bat and an honest approach always work best for you in relation to friendship.

15 MONDAY ☿ *Moon Age Day 8 Moon Sign Libra*

A variety of different sorts of news and views could be available to you at the beginning of this working week. Confidence shouldn't be difficult to find when you need it the most, but you will have to work especially hard to achieve a goal that you have definitely set your mind on. Conforming doesn't always come easily now.

16 TUESDAY ☿ *Moon Age Day 9 Moon Sign Libra*

This is one of your best days for freely pursuing personal interests. Today offers you a chance to blow a breeze of change into your life. The spotlight is on your level of general optimism and your willingness to put in whatever effort is necessary in order to gain your most cherished objectives.

17 WEDNESDAY ☿ *Moon Age Day 10 Moon Sign Scorpio*

Talking others round to your own particular point of view is part of what today is about. Be ready to use your good persuasive skills and plenty of charm to make the world your own. This is especially true in any professional situation, but can also be significant socially, once work is completely out of the way.

18 THURSDAY ☿ *Moon Age Day 11 Moon Sign Scorpio*

Your good ideas and definite ingenuity can be invaluable this week. Don't be afraid to offer your opinion if it is requested, and make the most of the rewards you can reap in return. Romance also counts for a great deal now, and could offer the odd surprise or two.

19 FRIDAY ☿ *Moon Age Day 12 Moon Sign Sagittarius*

What happens in the practical world today could prove to be quite decisive. Think carefully about any significant changes you wish to make at home, and about your expectations of how family members should behave. Your plans could come to very little unless you show that you have your finger on important pulses!

20 SATURDAY ☿ *Moon Age Day 13 Moon Sign Sagittarius*

A variety of new interests now assist you to get the very best from life. Try not to get overanxious about situations that don't really matter at all. Cultivate your more creative side and seek out intellectual stimulation. Trends suggest that cultural pursuits have the most to offer you this weekend.

21 SUNDAY *Moon Age Day 14 Moon Sign Capricorn*

Planetary trends are shifting all the time now and you need to be ready to face a day during which good co-operation is the key to success. It's not a question of putting yourself at the head of things at the moment. Rather, there are gains to be made by making sure you become part of a team.

22 MONDAY *Moon Age Day 15 Moon Sign Capricorn*

You now find yourself in a period during which you are encouraged to push ahead with all practical matters. Difficulties associated with relationships can be overcome at this time, and you can seek the sort of support you need from friends when you want it the most. This has potential to be a good start to the week.

23 TUESDAY *Moon Age Day 16 Moon Sign Aquarius*

You should be able to accomplish a great deal today. There are strong planetary forces available, in addition to the lunar high. Now is the time to identify what you want from life and then to go out and get it. Gathering support for any cause close to your heart should be child's play at present.

24 WEDNESDAY *Moon Age Day 17 Moon Sign Aquarius*

Today responds best to a completely confident approach, assisted greatly by the presence of the Moon in your own zodiac sign. If there are things you are bursting to say, now is the time. With the chance to tap into plenty of good luck at this time, you can afford to chance your arm a little more than usual.

25 THURSDAY *Moon Age Day 18 Moon Sign Pisces*

Trying to make the world run the way you wish is not to be recommended now. It would be far better for the moment to realise that your own opinions belong to you and that they might not be shared by others. Mistakes are a natural part of life, but what makes the difference is your ability to initiate a damage-limitation exercise.

26 FRIDAY *Moon Age Day 19 Moon Sign Pisces*

Some of your efforts in the outside world could slow down somewhat, leaving you feeling that you have reached a lull. Actually, this isn't the case, and you need to realise that a more thoughtful approach can help you to achieve more. Worries about the behaviour of younger family members might prove unfounded.

27 SATURDAY *Moon Age Day 20 Moon Sign Aries*

Relationships and personal encounters can prosper under today's trends. The Sun has entered your solar seventh house. As a result, material gains may be slightly more difficult to achieve for the next month, though all social and personal encounters are well accented. Your nature achieves a good balance.

28 SUNDAY *Moon Age Day 21 Moon Sign Aries*

You are now in a position to bring certain projects to a state of completion. This might not be too easy to achieve on a Sunday if the subject matter is professional, but you can ensure that progress is made in family-based schemes. Co-operative skills are emphasised, assisting you to get your head together with others.

29 MONDAY *Moon Age Day 22 Moon Sign Aries*

Don't settle for second best today, either from yourself or others. You really can afford to push situations now, even if you feel that in some cases you are going too far. It's time to let the true originality of your zodiac sign shine out like the sun. However, you can't expect everyone to approve of your approach.

30 TUESDAY *Moon Age Day 23 Moon Sign Taurus*

You needn't take no for an answer in situations about which you are absolutely certain. At the same time, a high degree of diplomacy can make all the difference. It's important to realise that you can't deal with everyone in exactly the same way. Listen carefully to what others have to say before you speak out.

31 WEDNESDAY *Moon Age Day 24 Moon Sign Taurus*

Be open and ready to seek new input at this time, especially from people who have been just outside your inner circle for some time. There is much to be said for making a few changes in terms of the people you mix with on a day-to-day basis, and there is a definite feeling of 'off with the old and on with the new'.

August

2013

1 THURSDAY *Moon Age Day 25 Moon Sign Gemini*

By all means spend time socialising today, though you need to avoid getting involved in disputes. Staying neutral is your best approach if possible, and you might even have to play the honest broker among friends. Events now may be interesting, though you have to steer a careful course if you don't want to become involved in contentious issues.

2 FRIDAY *Moon Age Day 26 Moon Sign Gemini*

Your strength lies in your ability to deal with tricky professional situations, some of which may need some very careful thought. Make sure you are getting enough rest at this time, and don't expect more of yourself than is reasonable. Help is there for the taking, but you will have to admit you need it first.

3 SATURDAY *Moon Age Day 27 Moon Sign Gemini*

If you've benefited from favours done by those close to you, today would be an ideal chance to find ways and means to pay them back. Attitude is all important if you need to deal with people who can be difficult. It is essential to remain patient and not to push situations more than is strictly necessary.

4 SUNDAY *Moon Age Day 28 Moon Sign Cancer*

Be prepared to deal with some ups and downs when it comes to personal finances. Once you start to realise that money isn't everything, it should become possible for you to get by on very little today. Even if you've taken this fact on board, any extra cash you can identify at present would be very welcome!

5 MONDAY *Moon Age Day 29 Moon Sign Cancer*

Current influences suggest that this is an ideal time to think seriously about life and to make some necessary changes. These need to take place first of all in your mind, and you won't move mountains in the real world until you have done so inside yourself. It really is a case of 'think it done and it is' right now.

6 TUESDAY *Moon Age Day 0 Moon Sign Leo*

Although you can create a happy and generally contented day, it might not be too eventful. The lunar low is influencing this state of affairs, though you needn't allow it to push you down into the doldrums. Why not get a change of scene, put on your best clothes and persuade friends to make the running?

7 WEDNESDAY *Moon Age Day 1 Moon Sign Leo*

Activities in the outside world may well appeal much more than things that are happening either at work or at home. That's why being with friends works well today, and is a chance to have a good time and make the most of the summer weather. Come to think of it, this would be an excellent period to take a holiday.

8 THURSDAY *Moon Age Day 2 Moon Sign Leo*

Even if you find it difficult to make progress now, there are still ways in which you can help yourself. For one thing, you need to avoid becoming involved in any schemes that you know in your heart are a waste of time. Confidence isn't lacking, though that isn't enough on its own to see you through. Creative potential is well accented.

9 FRIDAY *Moon Age Day 3 Moon Sign Virgo*

Your desire to make important changes is highlighted, but that doesn't mean it will be easy. Still, it's worth putting in that extra bit of effort if what you get out of it at the end is improving your life. Stand by to make a positive impression on individuals who are in an excellent position to offer you a boost.

10 SATURDAY *Moon Age Day 4 Moon Sign Virgo*

The most powerful emphasis today is on your professional life, which might be rather a waste of time to so many of you at the weekend. Of course there's nothing to stop you looking ahead and planning, though this might not be possible if you are busy in a social sense too. It's a question of fitting everything in.

11 SUNDAY *Moon Age Day 5 Moon Sign Libra*

It pays to bring a strong sense of movement into your life this Sunday by keeping yourself going, even if others are falling by the wayside. Energy is there when you need it the most, though you needn't be averse to putting your feet up either. Financial gains are by no means guaranteed at this time, but they are possible.

12 MONDAY *Moon Age Day 6 Moon Sign Libra*

Material restrictions might encourage you to cut back on one or two things, though probably not for long. In a way it shouldn't matter because what you want most from life at the moment cannot be purchased with any amount of cash. The emphasis is on your search for personal happiness, and today offers you scope to move towards it.

13 TUESDAY *Moon Age Day 7 Moon Sign Scorpio*

Organisation is the key to success now. If you really want to make the best of this period, trends encourage you to think well ahead and act with great decision this week. It might mean taking some things at a slower pace, but as long as you are thorough, you can make the most of any potential gains.

14 WEDNESDAY *Moon Age Day 8 Moon Sign Scorpio*

This is a time when you have what it takes to become the centre of attention and attraction. Part of this process is recognising how much you are admired by those around you, and it's up to you to pick up the relevant signals and information. Make sure you're not slow on the uptake now!

15 THURSDAY *Moon Age Day 9 Moon Sign Scorpio*

The spotlight now is on finance, particularly other people's money. This would be an ideal time to look at family investments, or offer some sound advice to those around you. Practical matters aside, it also pays to find time for enjoyment. August is growing older, but you need to show you have all the energy of a spring chicken!

16 FRIDAY *Moon Age Day 10 Moon Sign Sagittarius*

Once again, money matters are well accented, and financial planning is the order of the day. You need to show how astute you can be, especially when it comes to seeing all the different possibilities and strategies that are available to you. Aquarius is both confident and comfortable at the moment, and it should show.

17 SATURDAY *Moon Age Day 11 Moon Sign Sagittarius*

Although you can afford to pursue a high degree of personal freedom right now, it's worth getting important jobs out of the way before you think about taking a break. There's no need to sit on the fence in issues you know to be important. Even if it means disagreeing with a friend, you have to speak your mind.

18 SUNDAY *Moon Age Day 12 Moon Sign Capricorn*

Joint financial endeavours and co-operative ventures generally are well accented right now. Your intuitive powers are highlighted, assisting you to weigh up any given situation almost instantly. With a slight change of emphasis from yesterday you can make sure you show yourself to be a good talker, rather than a contentious individual.

19 MONDAY *Moon Age Day 13 Moon Sign Capricorn*

If you were planning on taking a chance in any romantic sense, now is the time to do it. Trends assist your attempts to win others round to your point of view, even beyond personal attachments. Fortune favours the brave, and you have scope to show more than a little courage for much of the coming week.

20 TUESDAY *Moon Age Day 14 Moon Sign Aquarius*

Make the most of the positive help you can obtain, and be ready to show that you know your own business best. Your desire to seek a change of scene could be very strong and is emphasised even more by the lunar high. What an excellent time this would be for Aquarius to take a holiday.

21 WEDNESDAY *Moon Age Day 15 Moon Sign Aquarius*

Now comes the chance to put longed-for plans and ambitions to the test. This can be very much your day, though it depends entirely on the amount of effort you are willing to put in. That shouldn't be a problem if you are raring to go. A cool exterior can make all the difference, even on those occasions when you are nervous inside.

22 THURSDAY *Moon Age Day 16 Moon Sign Pisces*

There are good reasons to deal with practical issues as quickly as you can, since this gives you the opportunity to do things that are simply for the sake of enjoyment. Don't feel guilty about this. If you've been putting in plenty of effort across the last couple of weeks, it's only fair that you also take some time to yourself.

23 FRIDAY *Moon Age Day 17 Moon Sign Pisces*

Doing things in pairs is the name of the game now. Co-operative ventures are favoured, no matter if these relate to your efforts at work, or your attempts to tackle personal attachments. You can't expect to be everyone's cup of tea today. The trick is to get the people who really matter on your side.

24 SATURDAY *Moon Age Day 18 Moon Sign Aries*

It pays to do more of your own thing today, as opposed to pleasing others all the time. This isn't really selfish, and even if it could be considered so, you do have the right to address your own life sometimes. Family rows are best avoided, especially if you are not the one who is starting them.

25 SUNDAY *Moon Age Day 19 Moon Sign Aries*

You are in a position to make today a good deal more exciting than you expected. If you work on a Sunday, look out for a chance to gain new power or responsibilities. However, if you have the weekend to yourself, the emphasis should be on making changes to your social life, and even taking a few calculated risks.

26 MONDAY *Moon Age Day 20 Moon Sign Taurus*

There is a continued accent on work and material considerations, so much so that you might find it difficult to spend any time doing exactly what you want. If you do manage to get some free hours, this could offer you the chance to give support to other people, particularly those who are having difficulties.

27 TUESDAY *Moon Age Day 21 Moon Sign Taurus*

It's worth devoting much more attention to practical situations now. This could leave you with little time today to concentrate on personal issues, or to consider the concerns of your friends. Getting involved in a range of activities is all very well, but taking on too much might create something of a panic.

28 WEDNESDAY *Moon Age Day 22 Moon Sign Gemini*

Look out for setbacks in the workplace and deal with them as soon as possible. It's natural to want to gather new information, though this isn't always recommended, and for now your interests are best served by concentrating on routine, even mundane, tasks. The ideal time for real change is still a few days off.

29 THURSDAY *Moon Age Day 23 Moon Sign Gemini*

Unlike yesterday, you are now encouraged to make use of information you can glean from others, so it is definitely worth keeping your ears open today. That shouldn't be too much of a demand because Aquarius can be one of the best dealers in gossip to be found anywhere within the zodiac. Be prepared to pursue small financial gains.

30 FRIDAY *Moon Age Day 24 Moon Sign Gemini*

This has potential to be a less demanding sort of day, allowing you to find at least some time to spend on your own. This isn't too unusual for Aquarius, and the quiet side to your nature assists you to take advantage of the opportunity. By the evening you can tap into a strong social trend that is now available.

31 SATURDAY *Moon Age Day 25 Moon Sign Cancer*

What matters about today is eliciting the right sort of assistance for whatever you are planning. Your astute nature and strong intuition can be brought into play and your decisions should now be quite considered. Even if you're happy to tackle routine tasks, there could still be a part of you that needs change and travel.

September 2013

1 SUNDAY *Moon Age Day 26 Moon Sign Cancer*

A feeling of self-fulfilment can really make the difference at present. Is there any point in continuing to do anything unless you can be sure that it will match up to your expectations of yourself? Where others are concerned, it's time to show the world at large just how gracious and generous you can be.

2 MONDAY *Moon Age Day 27 Moon Sign Leo*

Trends indicate that you can't expect to get your own way in everything now, since your perspectives are influenced by the presence of the lunar low. Rather than trying to do too much in a practical or material sense, this particular Monday would be an ideal time to do something that pleases only you.

3 TUESDAY *Moon Age Day 28 Moon Sign Leo*

It's time to ask yourself whether you are really in control of specific major personal issues in your life. There is no shame in seeking some timely advice, specifically from people who know a great deal about your life and circumstances. Despite the lunar low, there is much to be said for forging new friendships.

4 WEDNESDAY *Moon Age Day 0 Moon Sign Leo*

Tricky problem-solving is definitely assisted right now by the position of Mercury in your solar chart. You have what it takes to get to grips with any issues that you have been deliberately avoiding, and needn't allow yourself to be fazed by the behaviour of others. You can take on board some big issues now, and a positive attitude helps.

5 THURSDAY *Moon Age Day 1 Moon Sign Virgo*

Financially speaking there are good reasons to seek the support you need, when it is most required. Bear in mind that sometimes what seems like a backward step can prove to be necessary in a practical sense. Maybe you are starting to realise that new and innovative ideas are not always exactly what you need.

6 FRIDAY *Moon Age Day 2 Moon Sign Virgo*

Perhaps this isn't the best of times to gamble, particularly when it comes to activities that leave you little chance of winning anything. However, there are times when you are faced with a certainty, and you can afford to follow this all the way. Using your intuition is the best approach when assessing how others will behave.

7 SATURDAY *Moon Age Day 3 Moon Sign Libra*

The more determined edge to your nature returns, and you need to be ready to use it. When it comes to getting things right first time, you should have no problem at all. Confidence is emphasised again, and is assisted by the present position of the Sun in your solar eighth house. This is still a transitional period for you.

8 SUNDAY *Moon Age Day 4 Moon Sign Libra*

Minor financial gains are available, probably as a result of your own efforts rather than thanks to simple good luck. Once again you need to realise that, having made a decision, you need to stick to it, even if you feel this is at the expense of common sense. Doing things your own way can become an art form for Aquarius now.

9 MONDAY *Moon Age Day 5 Moon Sign Libra*

Present planetary trends encourage you to show your detective skills. By all means use them to find out what makes people tick, though you need to be somewhat careful that you aren't seen to be prying into people's lives. Creative potential could be going off the scale, and can be invaluable for making changes at home.

10 TUESDAY *Moon Age Day 6 Moon Sign Scorpio*

You are now in an ideal position to make some significant changes in your personal life. This is a time when you should be prepared to look at old matters in a very new light. All the same, you need to ask yourself whether you really are achieving major alterations or merely 'tinkering' with life.

11 WEDNESDAY *Moon Age Day 7 Moon Sign Scorpio*

Now you have a chance to catch up on unfinished business. Wednesday responds best if you find time to please yourself and are willing to take an innovative approach. Concern for the underdog is indicated, and you have scope to offer support to younger family members. Confidence is well accented.

12 THURSDAY *Moon Age Day 8 Moon Sign Sagittarius*

Your desire to look at things in a fresh manner is emphasised today. An element of boredom is possible regarding some of your actions, though you can still make progress by finding new ways to look at old problems. You might decide to leave tedious jobs until later or, better still, to persuade someone else to do them for you!

13 FRIDAY *Moon Age Day 9 Moon Sign Sagittarius*

With travel matters positively highlighted, this would be an ideal time to leave behind the stresses of everyday life and stay on the go. Even if you have been enjoying life to the full, you may have been putting yourself through the mill too much. Today offers an opportunity to relax more, which has to be positive.

14 SATURDAY *Moon Age Day 10 Moon Sign Capricorn*

There are signs that professional obligations could test your patience this weekend. If you are not at work, it pays to find ways to enjoy yourself beyond the confines of your own front door. The world has plenty to offer, so it's time to put some of your innovative ideas to the test. Getting on well with others should help.

15 SUNDAY *Moon Age Day 11 Moon Sign Capricorn*

Time spent at home has potential to be rather enjoyable today. You can afford to put your desire to mix and mingle to one side and show how willing you are to take life very steadily. This sudden change in direction is influenced by the temporary position of the Moon in your solar chart.

16 MONDAY *Moon Age Day 12 Moon Sign Aquarius*

The Moon moves into your zodiac sign, creating all the potential you need to make this a really positive sort of Monday. Not only can you increase your popularity among friends, you also can get yourself in the good books of family members. Most important of all, you know how to have fun and to inspire it in others.

17 TUESDAY *Moon Age Day 13 Moon Sign Aquarius*

You should still be in a position to capitalise on a little good luck, which could be found almost anywhere today. Be prepared to give your attention to people who demand it, though the individuals who hold particular interest for you right now are those with something significant to say.

18 WEDNESDAY *Moon Age Day 14 Moon Sign Pisces*

This would be a favourable time to look at the way your life is structured and make decisions about necessary changes. It's late in the year for a spring clean, but that in effect is what you have a chance to accomplish. Keeping hold of things simply for the sake of habit is not recommended. A slightly ruthless approach works well.

19 THURSDAY *Moon Age Day 15 Moon Sign Pisces*

Your intuition can now be invaluable in solving any problems you encounter today. Understanding what makes other people tick can help you to achieve some real gains. The sympathetic side of your nature is emphasised at present, as is your willingness to change your own direction in life a little in order to help someone else.

20 FRIDAY *Moon Age Day 16 Moon Sign Aries*

You could do a lot worse today than choosing to spread your wings. Even if travel hasn't been uppermost in your mind as much this year as it sometimes is, there are signs that wanderlust does begin to play a part in your thinking from now on. This would be an ideal time to take a holiday.

21 SATURDAY *Moon Age Day 17 Moon Sign Aries*

Once again you can capitalise on a period of change that is now available. It's worth considering whether certain friendships have run their course. If you don't want to hurt anyone, one option is to simply retreat from situations that no longer hold anything for you. Be prepared to give an explanation, even if it's not the whole truth.

22 SUNDAY *Moon Age Day 18 Moon Sign Taurus*

The Sun moves into your solar ninth house, which is particularly favourable for broadening your horizons and getting to grips with changes that are taking place at work. Socially speaking you have what it takes to get back on form, and should be ready to mix and mingle throughout most of the day.

23 MONDAY *Moon Age Day 19 Moon Sign Taurus*

The spotlight is now on your ability to dismiss challenges, even those that come thick and fast at work. When you have managed to climb a series of mountains to get what you want from life, remember that further peaks will be in view. Are you trying a little too hard? A slight reduction in pace can make all the difference.

24 TUESDAY *Moon Age Day 20 Moon Sign Taurus*

There are signs that emotional matters could become quite intense today, and you would be wise to avoid getting involved in any rows. You can't expect everyone around you to understand or fall in line with your point of view. A dollop of respect all round is the order of the day, and you can afford to set an example.

25 WEDNESDAY *Moon Age Day 21 Moon Sign Gemini*

A day to get out and about if you can – the further the better! This potentially quieter interlude would at least be an ideal time to visit places you haven't seen before. Likewise, you may decide that strangers are easier to get along with than people you have known for a long time. Be willing to tackle puzzles of one sort or another.

26 THURSDAY *Moon Age Day 22 Moon Sign Gemini*

Progress in money matters could help you to feel more secure. It's important to find ways of improving your finances, perhaps in some rather unexpected directions. Conforming to expectations could be rather difficult, particularly if you find specific routine tasks very boring at present.

27 FRIDAY *Moon Age Day 23 Moon Sign Cancer*

Positive highlights now surround personal attachments and all romantic encounters, thanks to the effect of Venus, the planet of love. This encourages a greater element of co-operation in interactions with your partner, or – if you are single – a better understanding of the needs of other people.

28 SATURDAY *Moon Age Day 24 Moon Sign Cancer*

Some self-sacrifice could be called for today, in order to offer support to someone you care about deeply. In the process, you might have to turn away from a situation you know would be advantageous. This needn't be a problem if you are willing to acknowledge that people come before any sort of material gain.

29 SUNDAY *Moon Age Day 25 Moon Sign Cancer*

Good company can help you to set this weekend apart. Your need to socialise is to the fore, and should allow you to put any worries to one side. By the time you get back to looking at certain situations you should feel they are far less intimidating, simply because you are refreshed by your willingness to do something different.

30 MONDAY *Moon Age Day 26 Moon Sign Leo*

It's time to slow the action and to take stock. The lunar low this time needn't be a particularly unfavourable interlude, nor does it require a pessimistic approach. What it does bestow is the chance to look at matters again, but this time with the addition of more common sense and circumspection.

October

2013

1 TUESDAY *Moon Age Day 27 Moon Sign Leo*

If it's difficult to gain a great deal in the way of assistance today, you might feel you are going it alone. Try to remember that much of what happens depends on your emotional state, which in turn responds to the lunar low. Slow and steady wins the race, even if this particular lap is not too eventful.

2 WEDNESDAY *Moon Age Day 28 Moon Sign Virgo*

Financial security is once again the focus of attention, and it's up to you to enhance your position in a range of different ways. An innovative approach could be the answer, and this would also assist you to leave behind everyday routines. Boredom has little to offer you under present planetary trends.

3 THURSDAY *Moon Age Day 29 Moon Sign Virgo*

You can afford to step up the pace of everyday life a notch or two, and to take advantage of some exciting situations, even if you have to manufacture some of these yourself. Individuals you haven't seen for some time, or even specific incidents, can prompt a renewed focus on the past. Be prepared to learn from this process.

4 FRIDAY *Moon Age Day 0 Moon Sign Virgo*

Today works best if you attract some good company, though this might be tricky if you are in a grumpy frame of mind! It's time to examine problems and identify how many are based in reality, and how many come from the recesses of your own mind. There's no point in worrying about situations you cannot alter.

5 SATURDAY *Moon Age Day 1 Moon Sign Libra*

A busy and hectic day is possible on the social scene, and you have scope to benefit from some enjoyable situations, even those that are rather unexpected. Getting involved in arguments is rarely a productive experience, especially if they involve your family or immediate friendship circle. Bear this in mind if tempers flare.

6 SUNDAY *Moon Age Day 2 Moon Sign Libra*

Communication issues are favourably highlighted now, and there are good reasons to speak to as many people as possible today in your efforts to get ahead generally. You needn't allow any barriers to prevent you from getting your message across intact, and your ability to persuade others to help you is noteworthy.

7 MONDAY *Moon Age Day 3 Moon Sign Scorpio*

Now comes the opportunity to broaden your horizons in ways that you may not have thought of before. It's a question of grasping any nettle firmly and taking the chance to push your influence with others. Any grandiose new schemes will work best if you can get others on your side, and you have the skills to do this.

8 TUESDAY *Moon Age Day 4 Moon Sign Scorpio*

It's important not to get too bogged down in technical matters today if you want to get ahead quickly. Of course, it would be madness not to take stock of safety issues and you need to realise this fact. However, if you can see any way of forging ahead through red tape, now would be an ideal time to give it a try.

9 WEDNESDAY *Moon Age Day 5 Moon Sign Sagittarius*

Getting down to brass tacks in your conversations with other people can make all the difference at this time. Diplomacy is all very well, though not if those around you fail to understand completely what you are trying to say. Fortunately, there is a middle path, and it's up to you to locate it.

10 THURSDAY *Moon Age Day 6 Moon Sign Sagittarius*

There is a strong emphasis on communications today, specifically when they relate to your dealings with younger people. They might think they have all the answers, but trying to bulldoze them with your own point of view is probably not the best approach. It pays to lead by example and show some patience.

11 FRIDAY *Moon Age Day 7 Moon Sign Capricorn*

Trends suggest that socially speaking you may be more reluctant than usual, and might be finding it difficult to take the initiative at the end of this working week. Are you simply regrouping your efforts and waiting for the right chance to push forward positively? On the other hand, a touch of laziness can't be ruled out!

12 SATURDAY *Moon Age Day 8 Moon Sign Capricorn*

The 'work hard and play hard' ethos of your sign should definitely be on display right now. You can afford to concentrate on those matters that are really important to your future and, when it is possible, to integrate your career and social life. Look out for all available opportunities to make a positive impression.

13 SUNDAY *Moon Age Day 9 Moon Sign Aquarius*

The lunar high is an excellent interlude for making fresh starts, and you need to recognise the potential of an improving situation. There are some definite gains to be made in material matters, and it's worth putting your general level of good luck to the test. An ideal time for entering into any sort of binding commitment.

14 MONDAY *Moon Age Day 10 Moon Sign Aquarius*

You may still be able to capitalise on some good luck as today gets underway. It is worth trying that bit harder to get what you want at work and to persuade other people generally that your point of view is sound and valid. Socially speaking, an open mind can work wonders, and unconventionality is the name of the game.

15 TUESDAY *Moon Age Day 11 Moon Sign Pisces*

There are some potentially lucrative ideas on offer now, and taking these on board should be a matter of pure instinct. Persuading others to go along with you may be more difficult, particularly if you have failed to think matters through as carefully as you should have. In at least one respect you can achieve a breakthrough.

16 WEDNESDAY *Moon Age Day 12 Moon Sign Pisces*

Seeking the bright lights of the social world can help you to cheer yourself up today. There are a number of astrological reasons to explain why you might be slightly down in the dumps, though you needn't allow these to spoil your day. Keep yourself in the mainstream at work and avoid unnecessary controversy.

17 THURSDAY *Moon Age Day 13 Moon Sign Pisces*

Be prepared to deploy some skilful manoeuvring in order to avoid disputes among those closest to you. Even if you can't make much material progress today, your ability to help others to sort out their problems counts for a great deal, and can help you to achieve a great deal of satisfaction.

18 FRIDAY *Moon Age Day 14 Moon Sign Aries*

This is a favourable day to be on the move and to say what you think, especially about practical situations. The real gains today might well be romantic. Prevailing trends assist you to strengthen new attachments, while you also have a chance to bring new zest and vitality to established relationships.

19 SATURDAY *Moon Age Day 15 Moon Sign Aries*

The best advice that can be offered to Aquarius today is to ensure that you get one task out of the way before you start on another. There is a danger of overlap and confusion, though not if you consider your actions carefully. You ought to be able to bring a good deal of happiness to family and friendship scenarios.

20 SUNDAY *Moon Age Day 16 Moon Sign Taurus*

Improved communication could well be the best gift of the weekend. There's no reason to be tardy when it comes to expressing an opinion, though you need to realise that not everyone will agree with you. Even if you aren't feeling absolutely positive about everything, the trick is to fool others – and even yourself!

21 MONDAY ☿ *Moon Age Day 17 Moon Sign Taurus*

All joint financial matters are especially well starred at present, as are partnerships with a monetary aspect. In addition, you have an opportunity to whisper those intimate little words that can make all the difference in the relationship stakes. Avoid being too quick to jump to conclusions in work matters.

22 TUESDAY ☿ *Moon Age Day 18 Moon Sign Gemini*

Signposts to success should be available now, though you will have to keep your eyes wide open in order to recognise them. Socially speaking there is much to be said for forging new friendships and even dispensing with some of your associations from the past. Aquarius is all about change and diversity at present.

23 WEDNESDAY ☿ *Moon Age Day 19 Moon Sign Gemini*

Making good progress with practical plans should leave you with time on your hands that can simply be used for having fun. Today is ideal for mixing with interesting people, particularly if they seem particularly keen to know you too. Affection can be gleaned from some very surprising directions.

24 THURSDAY ☿ *Moon Age Day 20 Moon Sign Gemini*

You can't expect to agree with everyone's opinions now, and you might even find some of them irrelevant or downright annoying. Rather than reacting too strongly, your best approach is to keep your cool. It is possible for you to score some singular successes, simply by refusing to rise to any bait that is presently offered.

25 FRIDAY ☿ *Moon Age Day 21 Moon Sign Cancer*

Career matters are now well accented. It pays to push ahead in educational activities, and to make the most of positive feedback. Home-based activities could be slightly less appealing, though you might have to turn your mind in that direction if it appears to be necessary.

26 SATURDAY ☿ *Moon Age Day 22 Moon Sign Cancer*

Progress in practical matters is once more supported, an indication that the position of the Moon can be particularly helpful ahead of the lunar low. Take the advantage it offers and make as much headway as you can. After that, be prepared to make the best of a couple of potentially slower days.

27 SUNDAY ☿ *Moon Age Day 23 Moon Sign Leo*

The lunar low is not necessarily a period of self-gain, though it really depends on the way you approach specific situations. Go slowly and steadily, weighing up the pros and cons in each case. The more carefully you address details, the greater is your chance of achieving success in the end.

28 MONDAY ☿ *Moon Age Day 24 Moon Sign Leo*

Once again a quiet and contemplative approach works best. Even if you don't personally see this as a problem, you need to ask yourself what other people are expecting of you. A willingness to explain yourself can make a difference, and in any case, the Moon will soon move out of Leo. Time for some delaying tactics?

29 TUESDAY ☿ *Moon Age Day 25 Moon Sign Leo*

Keeping your mind sharp and focused counts for a great deal now, and seeing ahead to the most distant horizon in your life should be a piece of cake. Be prepared to deal with any frustrations that arise from other people's actions. Bear in mind that their mistakes could lead to problems for you further down the line.

30 WEDNESDAY ☿ *Moon Age Day 26 Moon Sign Virgo*

You needn't be dissuaded from doing things your own way. Putting yourself out to accommodate the ideas of others is all very well, but going too far in this regard might not be to your advantage. When your intuition tells you to take a specific course of action, it would be sensible to heed it.

31 THURSDAY ☿ *Moon Age Day 27 Moon Sign Virgo*

In debates or discussions, you need to be ready to go up against people with strong egos at the moment. Remember that there is more than one way to skin a cat. If you remain absolutely charming and don't rise to the bait, you should be in a position to get your own way by default. Aquarius can be extremely cunning on occasions.

November
2013

1 FRIDAY ☿ *Moon Age Day 28 Moon Sign Libra*

You would be wise to stay away from speculation of any kind today, particularly before the middle of the day. By this afternoon, you have scope to create a much more positive atmosphere. It's not that trends have changed. Rather, it is a question of your own attitude, since you project your feelings on to the world at large.

2 SATURDAY ☿ *Moon Age Day 0 Moon Sign Libra*

Positive professional trends begin to make themselves felt. This is probably the best day of the week to concentrate on your work, though not exclusively. You need to be sure that colleagues understand what you are saying, even if this means labouring a point. Tedious chores shouldn't bother you too much now.

3 SUNDAY ☿ *Moon Age Day 1 Moon Sign Scorpio*

You can't expect your desire to please to be successful on all occasions, though that is no reason to avoid trying. The area of life that offers the best potential now appears to be that of romance. It's time to find the right words to say 'I love you', and to make the most of the response you attract.

4 MONDAY ☿ *Moon Age Day 2 Moon Sign Scorpio*

The progressive trends that have been on offer for a while now should continue, giving you scope to have more influence and a greater degree of control over the circumstances of your own life. It's worth seeking help from friends today, and this might even assist you in the direction of a much-cherished ambition.

5 TUESDAY ☿ *Moon Age Day 3 Moon Sign Sagittarius*

This is a particularly favourable time for social get-togethers of almost any sort. If you are willing to mix business with pleasure you can help yourself no end, and might even be able to gain in ways that are really surprising. Your naturally friendly manner is emphasised, and this assists you to show your best side.

6 WEDNESDAY ☿ *Moon Age Day 4 Moon Sign Sagittarius*

Being on the move can be quite rewarding. This is probably not a time to be standing still or to allow the grass to grow under your feet with regard to exciting new plans. You might be amazed at just how much work you can get through right now, particularly if you can obtain some timely assistance from friends.

7 THURSDAY ☿ *Moon Age Day 5 Moon Sign Capricorn*

This might not be the best day to pursue personal gain, though you should be able to make progress in other areas. For example, all romantic possibilities are highlighted, so it pays to focus your efforts there. Extra care is necessary in material matters. Whatever you are doing, once again it's worth asking friends for support.

8 FRIDAY ☿ *Moon Age Day 6 Moon Sign Capricorn*

Look out for good things that are happening on the social horizon and put yourself in a position to gain from them today. There are indications that your commitment to work could be lacking somewhat. However, that shouldn't prevent you from doing everything that is expected of you, and pitching in with advice when required.

9 SATURDAY ☿ *Moon Age Day 7 Moon Sign Aquarius*

Whatever is important in your personal agenda right now is what you ought to be chasing. The lunar high encourages you to go at problems with all guns blazing, and you needn't be distracted at this time. If you can get people to take notice of your opinions, even those who haven't been on your side before, so much the better.

10 SUNDAY ☿ *Moon Age Day 8 Moon Sign Aquarius*

Planetary benefits come along from a number of different directions while the lunar high continues. Now is the time to back your hunches and to seek to establish contact with someone you think of as being extremely special. Although the summer has now definitely passed, spending time out of doors can still work wonders.

11 MONDAY ☿ *Moon Age Day 9 Moon Sign Aquarius*

You may be throwing all your energy into getting exactly what you want from life. Bear in mind that this might appear to others to be a somewhat ruthless approach, though that isn't really the truth of the situation. Rather, if you have your heart set on certain goals, you won't take kindly to being diverted at all.

12 TUESDAY *Moon Age Day 10 Moon Sign Pisces*

There's no reason for you to go it alone at the moment. Progress today is a question of finding people who will lend a hand when you need it the most. If you do feel isolated, ask yourself whether the fault is your own. There are occasions when Aquarius is too proud for its own good, and today might be an example.

13 WEDNESDAY *Moon Age Day 11 Moon Sign Pisces*

Socially speaking this continues to be a period that offers you scope for fulfilment and the chance to get onside with people who haven't played a significant role in your life up to now. By all means listen to the plans of relatives and friends, especially if these concern you. However, it still pays to keep your options open.

14 THURSDAY *Moon Age Day 12 Moon Sign Aries*

Compromises made in social settings could prove to be especially important at this time. Trends assist you to express your feelings effectively at the moment, and to prove your sincerity to other people. Remember that strong emotions are a natural response to issues about which you feel strongly.

15 FRIDAY *Moon Age Day 13 Moon Sign Aries*

A careful approach works best with loved ones and intimates today. This probably isn't the time to display your knockabout sense of humour, and patience counts for a great deal, especially if you want to explain something to others. Be prepared to create interesting interludes for family members.

16 SATURDAY *Moon Age Day 14 Moon Sign Taurus*

Although you could be rather impatient with material obligations today, you will have to get these out of the way before you can begin to move forward in certain respects. It isn't so much what people need of you that can irritate, more what some of them 'expect'. It is very important to keep your cool.

17 SUNDAY *Moon Age Day 15 Moon Sign Taurus*

You can now afford to be yourself and to make room in your life for a few small, personal indulgences. An active approach is still the order of the day, though you also need to find interludes during which you can please yourself and yet manage to help others too. Diversity is important in personal interests.

18 MONDAY *Moon Age Day 16 Moon Sign Taurus*

There is an emphasis today on life's more playful aspects. Taking anything particularly seriously is not to be recommended, at least until after Wednesday. You may be able to use your offbeat sense of humour and off-the-wall attitude to boost your general popularity. What's more, this approach can help you to achieve a great deal.

19 TUESDAY *Moon Age Day 17 Moon Sign Gemini*

The fewer mistakes you make today, the better you should feel about life as a whole. Even if concentration isn't very easy, you have an opportunity to win through if you simply employ a degree of dogged determination. Be willing to go it alone if you can't secure co-operation from those around you.

20 WEDNESDAY *Moon Age Day 18 Moon Sign Gemini*

Listening to gossip is all very well, but a little care would be no bad thing. Bear in mind that some of what you hear today could be misleading, or even downright wrong. Why not opt for some fresh air if you can? Locking yourself inside the house today offers you few benefits, either mental or physical.

21 THURSDAY *Moon Age Day 19 Moon Sign Cancer*

Make the most of opportunities to start something new and interesting now. The more entertainment you can discover in life, the more headway you should be able to make. It's also time for you to enter a new period in terms of relationships, during which your ability to understand the motives of others is emphasised.

22 FRIDAY *Moon Age Day 20 Moon Sign Cancer*

The Sun is entering your solar eleventh house today. This encourages you to become more of a team player, for the next month or so at least. It pays to listen to what others are saying, and to appreciate the logic of their plans and schemes. Don't be swayed simply because it wasn't you who had the ideas!

23 SATURDAY *Moon Age Day 21 Moon Sign Leo*

The lunar low brings a planetary lull, just in time for Saturday morning. What bearing this has on your life really depends on your attitude. As long as you are willing to take comfort in small things, and are ready to shelve some of your most grandiose schemes for just a couple of days, you can make the best of this interlude.

24 SUNDAY *Moon Age Day 22 Moon Sign Leo*

It's still unlikely that you'll be pushing over any buses today, as the lunar low continues. What you do have is great intuition, and the ability to use it to your own advantage. There's no need to delay tackling specific jobs. Before overtaxing yourself with too much detail, though, consider how much of it matters in the greater scheme.

25 MONDAY *Moon Age Day 23 Moon Sign Leo*

Even if there are obstacles to be dealt with at work, you have a chance to move forward socially and romantically. Consideration for family members and friends should be second nature, though you might not always be able to help them to the extent you would wish. Despite the departing lunar low, the potential is favourable.

26 TUESDAY *Moon Age Day 24 Moon Sign Virgo*

Your charming and playful side is now to the fore. However, it's important that you don't become so distracted by fun and games that you fail to get on in a practical sense. Make full use of today's potential by looking at the possibility of making changes to your living environment.

27 WEDNESDAY *Moon Age Day 25 Moon Sign Virgo*

Trends suggest you need change and diversity, though it might not be easy to find either of these out here in the middle of the week. The responsibility is on you to get situations working out the way you wish, and you definitely have the power to do that. Physical exercise can certainly make all the difference.

28 THURSDAY *Moon Age Day 26 Moon Sign Libra*

Challenges and confrontations are now a distinct possibility, particularly if you are reluctant to sit back and simply accept situations. The spotlight is on the competitive side of your nature, and on your willingness to defend yourself before you have even been attacked. Learn how to count to ten.

29 FRIDAY *Moon Age Day 27 Moon Sign Libra*

It's worth paying attention to specific arrangements this Friday, to check for possible hitches. A flexible approach is the order of the day, and it's worth being prepared to reorganise things at the last minute. Bear in mind that you might not be able to rely on family members even if you really do need their positive input.

30 SATURDAY *Moon Age Day 28 Moon Sign Libra*

An element of reluctance when it comes to social activities is indicated today, which might not appear to bode well for the upcoming weekend. However, you needn't allow this to stop you mixing with people you know well. It's only natural to show a degree of reserve if you have to deal with virtual strangers.

December

2013

1 SUNDAY *Moon Age Day 29 Moon Sign Scorpio*

Work and professional matters should now offer you scope for fulfilment. Even if you don't have to toil professionally on a Sunday, you can capitalise on this trend by keeping yourself occupied. Physical activity is no bad thing, as long as you don't do the typical Air-sign trick and overdo it. Moderation in all things is the key.

2 MONDAY *Moon Age Day 0 Moon Sign Scorpio*

The focus now shifts to the social arena. If there are any invitations on offer today, grab them with both hands. Support from friends and relatives can assist you to get the very best out of any given situation. What won't help you is negativity, so you would be wise to stay away from anyone who exhibits such a trait.

3 TUESDAY *Moon Age Day 1 Moon Sign Sagittarius*

Stand by for a potentially busy period, but one that can offer opportunities for rewards, especially from a financial point of view. It's time to put in the hard work necessary in order to get ahead, even if not everyone around you is equally helpful. Confidence counts for a lot now, especially in the eyes of others.

4 WEDNESDAY *Moon Age Day 2 Moon Sign Sagittarius*

There are signs that your mind could be almost anywhere except on the task in hand today. Concentration is in short supply, and you might even decide to delegate certain tasks to others. Fortunately this is a very short interlude and does at least offer you the chance to think some matters through at length.

5 THURSDAY *Moon Age Day 3 Moon Sign Capricorn*

Even if you can't achieve everything you wish today, that shouldn't stop you trying. The fact is that your powers of communication are now emphasised, and so asking for what you want shouldn't be at all difficult. That Aquarian charm can be very useful to you now, and the people who count the most are unlikely to resist!

6 FRIDAY *Moon Age Day 4 Moon Sign Capricorn*

This is a time when a break from routine could work wonders. The twelfth-house Moon encourages a dreamier interlude than usual, and there is much to be said for taking things steadily. Even if others are pushing you to take specific action, you need to be clear that there is really no rush.

7 SATURDAY *Moon Age Day 5 Moon Sign Aquarius*

The lunar high assists you to be fighting fit and keen to make the best sort of impression. Once again the fly in the ointment is that you might find it difficult to obtain the help you need from other people. It's time to put your best foot forward at work, but leave time for the personal enjoyment that is on offer later in the day.

8 SUNDAY *Moon Age Day 6 Moon Sign Aquarius*

Despite the positive influences on offer, you still need to make sure of important details if your plans are to succeed. It can't be stressed enough now how important it is to check and double-check. Taking care now should give you the best chance of achieving a long-standing objective.

9 MONDAY *Moon Age Day 7 Moon Sign Pisces*

Relationships could well be something of a struggle to deal with at the beginning of this working week. In games of chance, or sporting activities, keeping your wits about you assists you to make great gains. Avoid gloating over your successes. It isn't necessary and only cheapens your winning streak.

10 TUESDAY *Moon Age Day 8 Moon Sign Pisces*

Your social life is still on a roll, and some Aquarians might even decide to start Christmas somewhat early this year. This would be an ideal day to focus on matters that are both interesting and educational, and it's important to take your time where new skills are concerned. Most important of all, realise how close the holidays are.

11 WEDNESDAY *Moon Age Day 9 Moon Sign Aries*

Professionally speaking, the present position of the Moon offers a more stable and easy-to-read phase. Contributing to your own eventual success shouldn't be difficult, even if you have half an eye on the festive period that lies before you. It pays to show how confident you are when dealing with matters you understand.

12 THURSDAY *Moon Age Day 10 Moon Sign Aries*

Success today is a question of keeping your eyes and ears open. All manner of opportunities are on offer, and you don't want to miss any of them. However, you need to take what others are saying with a pinch of salt, because it is entirely possible they are either joking, or trying to pull the wool over your eyes in some way.

13 FRIDAY *Moon Age Day 11 Moon Sign Taurus*

Your go-getting side is certainly to the fore today. With masses of energy, an original way of seeing things and plenty of charm, you should have little difficulty impressing some pretty important people. Although a favourable time socially speaking, today revolves primarily around work and practical issues.

14 SATURDAY *Moon Age Day 12 Moon Sign Taurus*

You can now afford to put some of your recent ambitions on the back burner and to go with the flow for most of the weekend. There is much to be said for thinking ahead to Christmas. Today is an opportunity to do some planning, while at the same time encouraging others to prepare well in advance.

15 SUNDAY *Moon Age Day 13 Moon Sign Taurus*

Ask yourself whether your love life is offering everything you would wish. If not, it is possible to pep things up with just a little effort on your part. There is also an emphasis on your physical well-being, and on what you are doing to improve it. Being willing to take things easily would be a useful first step in this direction.

16 MONDAY *Moon Age Day 14 Moon Sign Gemini*

Make the most of encounters with people who come new into your life, and be prepared to be inspired. Seeking advice from someone, somewhere would be no bad thing, and you would be wise to listen, even if you decide to follow your own path in any case. All in all, you have scope to make this a positive day.

17 TUESDAY *Moon Age Day 15 Moon Sign Gemini*

Simple conversation is what proves to be most useful today. It's up to you to gather inspiration from the things you hear as you go about from place to place, and to use this to come up with ideas that can mature in the fullness of time. It's important to recognise the limits of what you can do for other people.

18 WEDNESDAY *Moon Age Day 16 Moon Sign Cancer*

When it comes to organising your home life, co-operation is the key, and you need to show just how giving you can be. This could well be in stark contrast to the more practical qualities you possess. Bear in mind that this polarity in your nature might be difficult for some people to understand.

19 THURSDAY *Moon Age Day 17 Moon Sign Cancer*

This has potential to be a very inspiring day in almost every respect. Mercury strengthens its position in your chart, encouraging you to adopt a more sociable and tolerant attitude. This alone can help you to feel more comfortable, particularly as it is the way Aquarians operate for much of the time.

20 FRIDAY *Moon Age Day 18 Moon Sign Cancer*

This is a day on which you can afford to follow your instincts, which are unlikely to let you down. You can't expect everyone you meet at present to be equally reliable, so you need to be able to sort out the wheat from the chaff. Turn up your intuition and listen carefully to what it is telling you.

21 SATURDAY *Moon Age Day 19 Moon Sign Leo*

As the lunar low arrives, energy could be in short supply, so it pays to use it wisely. Avoid taking on unnecessary jobs or those which you know you have little chance of completing in a reasonable time. This is a day on which to pace yourself, take time to rest and be willing to seek a little help and support from those around you.

22 SUNDAY *Moon Age Day 20 Moon Sign Leo*

A rest period is the order of the day, and this Sunday offers all the right circumstances to get one. Don't rush your fences, and be willing to persuade others to take some of the strain. It's time to appreciate the friends who care about you deeply, as well as the relatives who are willing to put themselves out on your account.

23 MONDAY *Moon Age Day 21 Moon Sign Virgo*

Although Christmas is just around the corner, it might not be time to forget about work just yet. You need to look out for information on new and interesting responsibilities and opportunities. Even if these won't materialise before the New Year, you should still relish the prospect, and might even be starting to plan!

24 TUESDAY *Moon Age Day 22 Moon Sign Virgo*

Trends for Christmas Eve encourage you to keep up a fast pace, though you need to ensure you don't tire yourself out. Spread your efforts socially and don't focus your attention in any one direction. Your strength lies in your willingness to take account of all the people who deserve your time during this special season of the year.

25 WEDNESDAY *Moon Age Day 23 Moon Sign Virgo*

What enables you to set today apart is your ability and willingness to bring out the best in others. You could well have plenty to keep you busy, both inside the family and further afield. It might not be possible for you to achieve a totally stay-at-home Christmas Day, and you have plenty of scope for seeking excitement.

26 THURSDAY *Moon Age Day 24 Moon Sign Libra*

Gradually, trends are encouraging you to identify more with the needs and aspirations of the group and, as Christmas wears on, it pays to make the most of the interludes you spend with others. It's time to show the quirky side of the Aquarius nature, though in ways that make your relatives and friends smile.

27 FRIDAY *Moon Age Day 25 Moon Sign Libra*

It isn't friends but acquaintances that have most to offer you at the moment. The most casual conversations can have great significance for your future. This is an ideal time for Aquarius to come up with good ideas, since the Christmas break gives you the chance to look at some of them more closely.

28 SATURDAY *Moon Age Day 26 Moon Sign Scorpio*

The time is right for you to get about socially and to find new ways of enjoying yourself. You need to capitalise on what festive social occasions have to offer you, and to look for ways to pep up the romantic side of your life. Whatever your choice, life finds ways and means to accommodate you.

29 SUNDAY *Moon Age Day 27 Moon Sign Scorpio*

Your social life generally and your association with people you love especially can offer you scope to make today quite special. All the same, the quiet side of your nature is emphasised, and you might choose to spend some time watching an ancient movie, or maybe reading a good book. Nostalgia has a part to play in this day.

30 MONDAY *Moon Age Day 28 Moon Sign Sagittarius*

Are you feeling tempted to retreat somewhat from all the fuss and bother associated with the festive season? An hour or two spent on your own can really make the difference, especially now that the Sun is in your solar twelfth house. A deeper, perhaps more contemplative, Aquarian should presently be on display.

31 TUESDAY *Moon Age Day 29 Moon Sign Sagittarius*

Getting along well in group situations might not seem as easy now as it did only a few days ago. You have to adjust to that twelfth-house Sun, while at the same time ensuring you don't give the impression you are being aloof. All the same, getting New Year parties going with a swing should bring you a degree of satisfaction!

RISING SIGNS FOR AQUARIUS

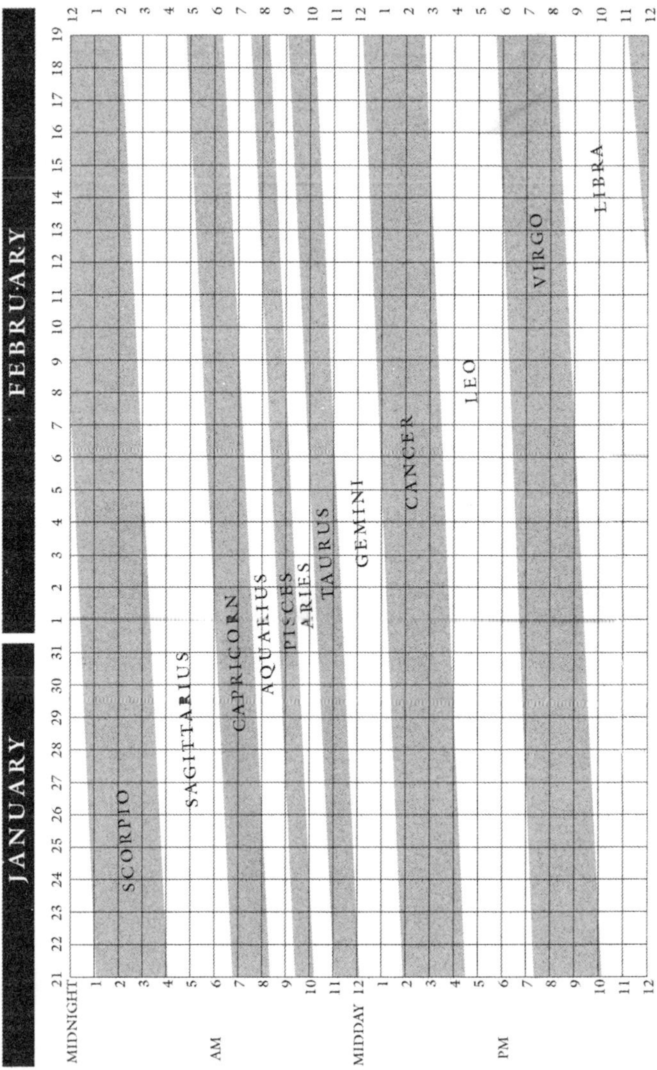

THE ZODIAC, PLANETS AND CORRESPONDENCES

The Earth revolves around the Sun once every calendar year, so when viewed from Earth the Sun appears in a different part of the sky as the year progresses. In astrology, these parts of the sky are divided into the signs of the zodiac and this means that the signs are organised in a circle. The circle begins with Aries and ends with Pisces.

Taking the zodiac sign as a starting point, astrologers then work with all the positions of planets, stars and many other factors to calculate horoscopes and birth charts and tell us what the stars have in store for us.

The table below shows the planets and Elements for each of the signs of the zodiac. Each sign belongs to one of the four Elements: Fire, Air, Earth or Water. Fire signs are creative and enthusiastic; Air signs are mentally active and thoughtful; Earth signs are constructive and practical; Water signs are emotional and have strong feelings.

It also shows the metals and gemstones associated with, or corresponding with, each sign. The correspondence is made when a metal or stone possesses properties that are held in common with a particular sign of the zodiac.

Finally, the table shows the opposite of each star sign – this is the opposite sign in the astrological circle.

Placed	Sign	Symbol	Element	Planet	Metal	Stone	Opposite
1	Aries	Ram	Fire	Mars	Iron	Bloodstone	Libra
2	Taurus	Bull	Earth	Venus	Copper	Sapphire	Scorpio
3	Gemini	Twins	Air	Mercury	Mercury	Tiger's Eye	Sagittarius
4	Cancer	Crab	Water	Moon	Silver	Pearl	Capricorn
5	Leo	Lion	Fire	Sun	Gold	Ruby	Aquarius
6	Virgo	Maiden	Earth	Mercury	Mercury	Sardonyx	Pisces
7	Libra	Scales	Air	Venus	Copper	Sapphire	Aries
8	Scorpio	Scorpion	Water	Pluto	Plutonium	Jasper	Taurus
9	Sagittarius	Archer	Fire	Jupiter	Tin	Topaz	Gemini
10	Capricorn	Goat	Earth	Saturn	Lead	Black Onyx	Cancer
11	Aquarius	Waterbearer	Air	Uranus	Uranium	Amethyst	Leo
12	Pisces	Fishes	Water	Neptune	Tin	Moonstone	Virgo